ROMAN SPECTACLE
— ON THE —
RIO GRANDE

ROMAN SPECTACLE
— ON THE —
RIO GRANDE

BORDERLAND ANIMAL FIGHTS AT THE TURN OF THE CENTURY

BRADLEY FOLSOM

THE
History
PRESS

Published by The History Press
Charleston, SC
www.historypress.com

First published 2024

Manufactured in the United States

ISBN 9781467155335

Library of Congress Control Number: 2023946798

Notice: The information in this book is true and complete to the best of our knowledge. It is offered without guarantee on the part of the author or The History Press. The author and The History Press disclaim all liability in connection with the use of this book.

For Elizabeth.

CONTENTS

ACKNOWLEDGEMENTS

While in graduate school, I kept a blog in which I researched and wrote about interesting and obscure true stories that I'd stumbled across during my coursework. I usually focused on subjects that I wanted to know more about but had somehow escaped the attention of the internet. One such post concerned a series of cage fights that took place on the Texas-Mexico border in 1895 involving a lion named Parnell, a grizzly named Ramadan and a bull named Panthera. Another entry discussed a 1907 battle between an American buffalo and a fighting bull in a Juárez bullring.

In the more than ten years since I wrote about these events, various podcasts, Reddit threads and other corners of the internet have mentioned the border animal fights, but to my surprise, no one had investigated them in greater detail than what was in my blog. Nor had anyone looked into the individuals who put on the fights or asked what the fights say about the broader issues facing the border at the turn of the century. Urged on by friends and family (who found the border battles much more interesting than the history I normally write about), I decided to revisit my old blog posts and expand on them for a book. In doing so, I found even more fascinating characters and unexplored stories than I could have ever anticipated.

I want to express my appreciation to my friends and family who encouraged and supported me during the writing process. Thanks go to Elizabeth Niedrauer, Mabel Folsom, Jason Lowrey, Joe Valdez, Kenny Burke, Tobias Deckard, Richard Mowrey, Geoff Folsom, Maria Folsom, Donald Chipman, Will Yancey, Josh Campbell, Ryan Hamzeh, Heather Folsom,

Gustav Monteblanc, Sarah Crain, Beau Bellett, Tom Ginsberg, Michael Gruber, Sarah Niedrauer, T.C. Fleming, Marshall Lilly, Will Evans, Andrew Mueller and Pawel Goral.

I would also like to thank Ryan Schumacher, William Hansard, Sandra Niedrauer and F. Todd Smith for reading early drafts of the manuscript and suggesting improvements. My press editors Ryan Finn and Ben Gibson were also helpful in this regard. David LaFevor and Danny Gonzalez assisted with various aspects of research, as did the staff of the Border Heritage Center of El Paso, the Texas State Library and Archives and the Special Collections department of the University of Texas–El Paso library. Perhaps more than any other, the late Randolph Campbell deserves credit for providing me with the tools to research and write about nineteenth- and twentieth-century history.

INTRODUCTION

From 1895 to 1913, promoters on the Texas-Mexico border imported a variety of large mammals from throughout the world to pit them against each other in interspecies combat. The various fighters included a tiger from the jungles of India, lions from the African savannah, an elephant from Siam, bulldogs from England, American bison from the North American Plains, coyotes from New Mexico, grizzly bears from California and Jalisco, a leopard from Africa and the very best fighting bulls of Sonora and Durango. Human combatants also occasionally entered the fray against the large mammals. In El Paso and Juárez, wrestlers grappled bulls, a rodeo pioneer submitted an elk and a bullfighter tried to combat a buffalo in the same manner he would a bull.

The events usually took place on the Mexican side of the border owing to recent legislative changes in Texas. In the late nineteenth century, the United States was amid the Progressive era, wherein an emerging educated middle class encouraged local and state governments to outlaw what they saw as uncivilized and unchristian aspects of society. Under pressure from progressive organizations, including the American Society for the Prevention of Cruelty to Animals (ASPCA) and the Humane Society, the State of Texas outlawed bullfighting in 1889, and numerous county and city governments followed suit with laws against cockfighting, dogfighting and other fight sports involving animals. The bans mattered little to most Texans because their preferred fight sport was human-on-human boxing. Unfortunately for boxing fans, progressives also saw prizefighting as

Fight sports involving animals were much more popular in Mexico than they were in the United States. The Spanish introduced bullfighting to Mexico during the colonial era, and it remained a popular sport throughout the nineteenth century. Bearbaiting was an adaptation of bullfighting common in northern Mexico, wherein vaqueros captured a local bear and forced it to combat a bull. *From* The Graphic: An Illustrated Weekly Newspaper, *December 30, 1876.*

uncivilized, and in 1895, they encouraged the governor of Texas to outlaw boxing, scuttling a match between heavyweights Bob Fitzsimmons and Jim Corbett set to take place in Dallas.

When Fitzsimmons and Corbett tried to move their bout to Juárez, Mexico, they discovered that Mexican president Porfirio Díaz had also recently outlawed human-on-human prizefighting. Few in Mexico at the time cared for boxing, and Díaz saw the measure as a means of improving his country's image abroad. However, Díaz did not ban cockfighting, bullfighting, bearbaiting, bullbaiting or any fights involving animals. These events held cultural and historical significance to Mexicans, and Díaz believed that the entertainment placated Mexico's lower classes. This meant that while a human could fight an animal and an animal could fight an animal in Juárez, Fitzsimmons and Corbett could not fight each other.

These legal circumstances led to a nearly two-decade period wherein opportunists on the border organized fights between large mammals for the purpose of selling tickets to American audiences. Owing to industrialization, many in the United States had expendable capital, but because of historical Puritanical influences and a belief in parity, few Americans wanted to spend their money in Mexico watching bullfights where matadors almost always emerged victorious. Therefore, some entrepreneurs sought to relieve the Americans of their dollars by making bullfighting more accessible and appealing to their sensibilities, while others tried to combine bullfighting with sports familiar to American audiences. Still others recognized that Americans wanted novelty and parity, leading them to put on battles between different species of animals that were perceived as equally vicious.

To appeal to the American desire for luxury and consequence, promoters advertised their events as a return to the days of ancient Rome, a time when emperors imported animals from throughout Africa, Asia and Europe to fight for the entertainment of large crowds in Roman coliseums. The animals and humans who fought in bullrings in Mexico became gladiators in advertisements. A cage fight featuring a tiger, bear and bull in Juárez was stylized as a "fight to the death between the gladiators of the wilds."[1] African American boxer Billy Clarke branded himself the "Chief of the Gladiators" and the "Colored Hercules" to sell tickets to his fights against lions, bulls and horses.[2] A promoter marketing a fight between a lion and a bull promised "one Brief Hour in a Roman Amphitheatre," "a grand spectacle" and "a Roman Holiday."[3]

Journalists adopted the Roman theme when writing about the events, and newspapers brought their detailed accounts of the fights to readers throughout the world. The late nineteenth and early twentieth centuries was a time of so-called yellow journalism, when newspaper purveyors sought out dramatic, violent and morbid stories to sell newspapers to audiences more interested in entertainment than thought-provoking journalism. Stories about bears fighting lions and a man wrestling a bull certainly fit with this new sensational style. The border therefore became "Nero's Playground" and the events a "revival of the sport of gladiator days of Rome."[4]

Advertisements and media attention drew crowds seeking the peculiar and the macabre to bullrings on the Mexican side of the border, with audiences sometimes exceeding ten thousand. Some events lived up to the hype and were awe-inspiring. When unleashed in the arena, the animals often sprang at each other with wanton abandon. Spurred by instinct or frightened into action by the roaring crowd, the animals used claws, teeth and horns to eviscerate their opponents and let loose entrails. Viscera and gore might

Roman mosaic featuring examples of spectacles seen in ancient coliseums. The Romans imported lions, tigers, rhinoceroses, elephants and even a polar bear to fight gladiators or other animals. *Wikimedia Commons.*

litter the floor of the bullring when fights were done. Other times, animals struggled to understand, much less combat, a supposed enemy their species had never encountered in the wild and were therefore hesitant to engage, even when pike-wielding attendants and toreadors prodded them to fight. Disappointed crowds often demanded their money back or refused to leave until one or both animals were dead.

This book will chronicle the various animal fighting spectacles that took place on the Texas-Mexico border from 1895 to 1913, focusing on the novel events meant to attract American audiences. It will also tell the stories of the eclectic people who staged the fights. Promoters included vaudevillian villain Daniel Boone, who claimed to be descendent of frontiersman Daniel Boone; French bullfighter and opportunist Felix Robert; American conservationist Scotty Philip, who wanted to save the buffalo from extinction; and Aboriginal Australian Bill Badger, who, as his adopted name implied, was as mean as a badger. The book will also discuss the animals involved in the fights, many of which also had vibrant personalities. Combatants included Ned, the ornery alcohol-imbibing elephant; Panthera, the proud bull; Parnell, the fierce lion; and Ramadan, the stalwart grizzly.

In telling the story of the events and the people and animals involved in them, the book will help explain the historical circumstances surrounding the fights. The late nineteenth and early twentieth centuries was a time of patriotism, paternalism, imperialism and progressivism in the United States, and the fights were influenced by and reflected American politics and culture in myriad ways. The history of Mexico can also be seen in the spectacles. At the dawn of the twentieth century, Mexicans were growing resentful of the increased American interference in their economy and politics, and because of this, the fights sometimes took on nationalistic overtones, especially when a "Mexican" fighting bull took on an animal that was perceived to be American, such as a grizzly or an American bison.

The purpose of this book is not to glorify the spectacles that took place on the Texas-Mexico border, nor is it meant to serve as a comprehensive history of interspecies fighting. Instead, the book is a series of unusual true stories that serve as reminders of the remarkable animals and people who participated in the fights and a chronicle of the efforts of those who tried to have them stopped. Moreover, the fights illustrate the thorny, complex relationship between the United States and Mexico and the uneven exchanges that often play out in borderlands entertainment. Finally, the political, social and economic context of the fights is fascinating. Studying them provides insight into a unique time and place in history.

CHAPTER 1

THE LION, THE BEAR AND THE BULL (PART I)

On April 1, 1895, American businessmen, Mexican elites, local officials, soldiers, vaqueros and vendors selling cold drinks filed into the Plaza de Toros bullfighting arena in Nuevo Laredo, Mexico. Sitting just across the border with the United States, the bullring had been prepped for a spectacle. Red, white and green Mexican flags hung throughout the arena, as did the smell of sweat and manure. It was hot, and those unable to afford a seat in the shade suffered in the desert sun.

The unpleasant heat and smell did little to dull the excitement of the upcoming event, as the people in the arena were about to witness something reminiscent of the days of Ancient Rome. Two of the largest mammals on earth were about to face off in a steel cage match. A 700-pound American grizzly sat in the center of the bullring, confined within a fifteen-foot-high, thirty-foot-wide steel cage draped in canvas. The bear's opponent, a 550-pound African lion, was locked in a pen outside of the arena.

When the designated fight time arrived, the lion's owner used pokers to prod the lion out of his pen and into a portable cage, which he then wheeled into the bullfighting ring and placed flush against the entryway to the bear's cage. The crowd gasped audibly upon viewing the jungle cat for the first time, most having never seen such an animal before. The lion broke the silence with a loud roar, which the crowd met with cheering and hollering. When attendants removed the canvas from the fighting cage, revealing the lion's grizzly bear opponent, the spectators grew louder. The noise and the sight of the boisterous audience agitated and scared both caged beasts. They seemed to want to take out their anger and fear on anyone or anything that they could get their paws on.

When a trainer opened the door separating the two animals, the lion immediately leaped fifteen feet into the air and came down directly on top of his grizzly opponent. The bruin, standing on his hind legs, caught the lion as it landed and used his forepaws to hold the cat's teeth away from its neck. The bear could do nothing, however, to stop the lion's claws from tearing into its midsection. Fur and blood flew everywhere.

Fortunately for the bear, its thick hide prevented the lion from reaching vital organs, but the grizzly was slow and every attempt to bite and claw the lion failed. The jungle cat was simply too quick. To those in attendance, it looked like the lion would eventually wear down the bear with its claws. After the animals held their upright position for nineteen minutes, the grizzly seemed to realize that it was much stronger and heavier than its opponent. Using its powerful arms, the bruin grabbed the lion and squeezed with all its might. The beast then created torque with its muscular back and tossed the jungle cat into the air, the lion

Artist depiction of the lion and bear fight in Nuevo Laredo on April 1, 1895. *From* The Inquirer, *February 12, 1905.*

turning a complete somersault before landing on its feet in the center of the cage. The fight was on.

The two animals belonged to Colonel E. Daniel Boone, an amiable, six-foot-two, broad-shouldered vaudeville performer who had come to Mexico out of desperation. His lion had just killed a man, and he needed to get rid of it. As a showman, Boone had concluded that a fight with a bear would be the most entertaining and profitable means to carry out this goal.

Like many late nineteenth-century circus performers, Boone had a backstory so spectacular that it is difficult to tell what parts of it were genuine and what parts he made up to impress paying audiences. Boone claimed to be the great-grandnephew of American frontiersman Daniel Boone, from whom he received his name.

Vaudeville promoter E. Daniel Boone. Boone often told conflicting stories about his past. When speaking to one reporter, he said that he lost part of his bicep after a lion attacked him in Africa but told another that the wound came from a trained lion biting his arm during a show in Chile. *From the Courier-Journal, February 5, 1898.*

Although there are reasons to question this assertion, there is little doubt that, like his namesake, Boone had led an interesting life. Born in Kentucky and raised in Louisiana, Boone served in the Confederate army during the Civil War, earning the rank of lieutenant colonel by 1865. After the war, Boone tried growing tobacco in Lynchburg, Virginia, but gave up the profession after a small circus passed through town and offered him a job as an elephant tamer—its pachyderm tossed the last person to hold the job. After a few years with the outfit, a time during which he began training lions, Boone joined Wilson's Circus just as it was departing for a tour of South America. During the trip, Boone took a job at a zoo in Peru, where he met and married his wife, New York–born Carlotta. The couple would have two children.

Apparently, married life and fatherhood did little to slow Boone down, as he spent the following decades engaged in both animal-related and military activities. He supposedly served as a military adviser to the government of Peru before joining a group of Americans under former Confederate general Thomas Jordan in trying to overthrow Spanish rule of Cuba. After failing in this endeavor, Boone set off for Europe, where he gave small exhibits as an animal trainer in Spain, France, Turkey and Egypt. Boone even came to the attention of the sultan of Turkey, who, after witnessing one of the trainer's lion shows, hired the American to serve as an advisor to the Turkish army. At one point, Boone went to Algeria, where he fought with the French army against a local insurrection.

While in Algeria, Boone joined an expedition led by Charles Bombonnel, a famous French lion hunter who made a living capturing African cats to sell to circuses. Bombonnel taught Boone how to capture lions by tying a calf to a weak structure over a bell pit. When a lion leaped on the calf, the structure would collapse, sending the animals to the bottom of the pit, where the lion could then be safely lured into a box for transport. Boone began using this process to capture lions to sell to circuses, but he soon found out that it was not foolproof. While Boone was watching a trap, a lion snuck up on him and bit a chunk out of his bicep. Fellow hunters managed to kill the lion before it could kill Boone, but the trainer would be missing a chunk of his bicep for the rest of his life. Setting aside this miscue, Bombonnel's method was successful, and Boone captured dozens of lions, some of which he sold to American circus owner P.T. Barnum. He began training others he captured, including a three-year-old male named Parnell, to serve as performers in his own lion taming act.

Boone developed several tricks over his years of lion taming. Using his whip and his German boar hound as negative reinforcements, he taught his lions what was by then the standard routine of having the felines jump through hoops and balance themselves on seesaws. More impressively and unique to his shows, Boone trained his lions to ride tricycles, pull Roman chariots and hold jump ropes for his boar hound to jump over. Perhaps his most famous trick was to have his wife, Carlotta, stick her head in an open lion's mouth. Newspapers lauded Boone's shows, calling them "the most astonishing exhibition of man's supremacy of human intelligence and courage over even the fiercest specimens of the wild animals of creation," and in 1891, the Adam Forepaugh Circus hired the trainer to perform as one of its main attractions.[5] For the next two years, Boone remained with Forepaugh, often entertaining audiences numbering in the tens of thousands.

By 1893, Boone had enough money to open his own touring vaudeville show, which he stocked with performing wolves, bears, gorillas, monkeys, leopards and tigers in addition to his famous lions. Problems plagued the show. Once, after Boone changed clothes between performances, one of his lions got confused, thought Boone was a stranger and tackled him. The trainer managed to calm the lion before he was hurt, but in another instance, an angry cat forced Boone to flee from the cage. Boone was lucky. One of his trainers would not be.

Boone took his animal exhibit to the San Francisco Midwinter Fair in January 1894. Everything proceeded normally for the fair's first two weeks, but during a performance on February 14, there was a power outage while attendant Carlo Thiemann was repairing the lights in the lion cage. During the blackout, the lion Parnell, which had grown to be 550 pounds since Boone captured him in Africa, grew scared at the noise the crowd was making in the dark and leaped on Thiemann, clawing and biting him repeatedly. The two other lions soon joined in on the assault. Boone reacted quickly, grabbed a lion prod, entered the cage, forced the animals away from the attendant and dragged Thiemann to safety, but the attendant had lost too much blood. He died of his injuries soon after arriving at the hospital.

At first, Boone ignored the fact that his lion had killed a trainer and continued to use Parnell in his shows. Unfortunately, the lion continued to be a problem. Less than a month after Thiemann's death, Parnell broke out of his cage and killed a small performing bear in a neighboring enclosure. During a different show, Parnell grabbed Nero, one of Boone's favorite boar hounds, and began to tear into the animal. Boone attempted to scare Parnell into letting the dog go by firing his pistol near the lion's head, but it was to no avail. Parnell only released the half-dead dog when Boone grabbed a heavy iron bar and beat the lion.

It did not take long for Parnell's reputation for violence to scare away ticket buyers, and many in San Francisco called on the trainer to euthanize the man-killing animal. Boone realized that he could no longer use Parnell in his shows, but he found the idea of throwing away the life of a $5,000 animal distasteful, especially considering that he was facing financial woes. Feeding and caring for a large cadre of animals cost money—as did paying trainers, attendants and ticket takers—and Boone seems to have been spending more than his shows were taking in. Boone's shaky financial situation also apparently owed to his gambling habits, as the colonel rarely turned down a bet.

Needing cash and unwilling to euthanize an expensive animal, Boone came up with a plan: he would stage a death match between Parnell and an American grizzly bear. It is unclear where Boone came up with the plan. Perhaps the lion escaping its cage and killing the small bear sparked his imagination. As a fan of history, he may have known about the spectacles put on by the Romans or the staged fights between bears and bulls that took place in California earlier in the nineteenth century. It is also possible that, having traveled extensively, he had seen a similar fight in Europe. In Paris in 1893, for example, a showman staged a fight between a polar bear and an African lion, with the jungle cat easily besting his larger opponent. Perhaps Boone simply wondered who would win between a grizzly and a lion. After all, the separation of the continents millions of years in the past meant that such a fight had never happened before.

It is also possible that Boone had fought animals before. He would later claim that his lions had earned him $32,000 by dispatching bulls in a series of fights in Chile. Although there is much about this claim that is questionable, if true, Boone would have prior experience earning money from animal fighting. Whatever his motivation, in March 1894, Boone made it be known that he planned to rent the midway of the San Francisco fairgrounds and hold the fight before the end of the fair. He also paid for the construction of a steel cage and stands and bought ad space in newspapers throughout California. The event's biggest expense, however, would be providing an opponent for Parnell.

Accounts of the bear's origins differ. Most sources agree that the animal was a male North American Brown Bear, also known as a grizzly or silvertip bear. Some sources place the bear's birthplace in the Rocky Mountains, others in California. If it was the latter, it might mean the bear was one of the last remaining California Golden Bears, a subfamily of grizzlies that went extinct in 1922. If this were true, the bear would not only be the first American grizzly to fight a lion, but the last California Golden Bear to do so. Wherever he was born, the grizzly weighed about seven hundred pounds, average size for brown bears, and like all grizzlies, it had razor-sharp claws and teeth, traits developed for tearing apart moose, elk, bison, smaller black bears and other prey.

It is unclear how Boone came to be in possession of the bear. The trainer may have taken the grizzly from his own cadre of trained animals. One newspaper reported that the animal was relatively gentle, raised in captivity, and had never killed another living creature, indicating that the animal belonged to a traveling show. A different account said that the bear was raised in captivity but had recently killed two of his trainers and, like Parnell, faced euthanasia for its actions. If true, the fight would be between two man-killers. Perhaps the most plausible origin story was that Boone simply requisitioned a hunter to find an animal for him in the surrounding countryside. Whatever the circumstances, when the bear came into Boone's possession, he began calling it Ramadan, a reference to the Muslim holy month and a likely callback to the time Boone spent in Turkey and North Africa.

Boone planned to stage the fight between Ramadan and Parnell on April 21, 1894. The showman took preorders on tickets, charging twenty dollars apiece. Even though this was a substantial sum of money in 1894, as soon as Boone announced the fight, tickets began "selling like hot cakes," and within a week, the event had sold more than one thousand seats. The high ticket prices irked one newspaper columnist, who lamented that society had degraded to a point where people refused to pay ten dollars for an opera or a play, but would put up twice that amount to see two four-footed brutes scrap. The columnist closed his editorial by asking sarcastically, "Who says we are not living in an intellectual, refined age?"[6] A second writer compared the upcoming event to the spectacles put on by the maligned Roman emperor Nero, while a third condemned the contest but could not resist betting on the bear to win.

Newspaper writers were not the only ones opposed to Boone's upcoming show. A group called the American Society for the Prevention of Cruelty to Animals (ASPCA) began petitioning the mayor of San Francisco to put an end to the event. Made up of concerned progressives who abhorred violence to animals incapable of defending themselves, the ASPCA was a powerful nationwide lobby that had supporters in the California legislature and Washington, D.C. Citing animal cruelty laws already on the books in California, they demanded that Boone be arrested, along with anyone who attended the event. The Humane Society joined in the protests.

Boone responded to the accusations of animal cruelty by saying that he was doing nothing wrong, as "there is no law to prevent him putting the animals in the same cage: then, if they happen to get mad and fight he will be perfectly willing to allow the member of the society and officers to go in and stop them."[7] When this excuse failed to alleviate the ASPCA's concerns, Boone attempted to argue that the proposed fight was simply a "wrestling match" between the two animals.[8] Unfortunately for Boone, the mayor of San Francisco did not agree with his assessment of the exhibition and was sympathetic to the ASPCA's cause. He therefore ordered the local police to the fairgrounds to tear down the animal fighting arena and demanded Boone refund any tickets he had sold.

In the hopes of recouping some of the money spent advertising the bear-versus-lion showdown, Boone arranged for famed strongman Eugene Sandow to fight a small lion, advertising the event as "man vs beast." The show was a dud. The lion was almost certainly drugged and appeared lethargic in the ring. It had also had its claws padded and its mouth taped to avoid injuring Sandow. The strongman did the best he could to elicit excitement from the crowd—at one point picking up the lion, swinging it and pinning it to the mat—but the lack of true danger left the crowd disappointed. Many demanded a refund on their tickets, putting Boone further in the financial hole.

Undeterred, Boone decided to try to move the bear-lion fight out of San Francisco to the nearby Vallejo Racetrack. The event was to be held on the Fourth of July and was expected to draw twenty thousand spectators. Once again, however, the proposed event was canceled after the county charged Boone with "attempting to bring off a fight between the lion and the bear."[9] Boone attempted to argue that animal cruelty laws were not applicable because the animals were not domestic, but the event's cancelation indicates that the county court did not accept this argument. It is also possible that the Society for the Prevention of Cruelty to Animals caught the governor's ear and had him outlaw the fight throughout California.

THE KING OF BEASTS HUNG IN HIS ARMS LIKE A SICK KITTEN.
[From a sketch by an "Examiner" artist.]

Eugene "The Great" Sandow was a vaudeville entertainer who lifted weights and flexed his muscles for paying audiences. Many credit his performances with popularizing bodybuilding worldwide, and the Mr. Olympia competition still awards a statue of Sandow to contest winners. Even the Great Sandow could not make wrestling a drugged lion entertaining. *From the San Francisco Examiner, May 23, 1894.*

Unable to find a venue for Parnell and Ramadan's bout in California, Boone packed up his animal show in late 1894 and moved to Texas, where he tried to fight the animals in Fort Worth. Before the bout could take place, a local judge deemed that the exhibition not only violated animal cruelty laws, but that it was also too risky to spectators and ordered it canceled. Whether specifically seeking a new location for a fight or following his circus's already established route, Boone brought his show to Laredo in March 1895. There, Boone made the decision to transfer his interspecies fight across the border to Nuevo Laredo, Coahuila, where there was no local version of the Society for the Prevention of Cruelty to Animals to stop the show.

Boone rented out the Plaza de Toros bullfighting ring in Nuevo Laredo to host the fight. Although it was the biggest arena in the border town, the Plaza de Toros could only seat 650 people, much fewer than would have been in attendance if the fight had been held in San Francisco or Fort Worth. Boone had no other option, however, so he oversaw the construction of fifteen-foot-high, twenty-foot-wide steel cage in the center of the bullring. He also sent notice to local newspapers that he was putting on a fight to the death between an American grizzly and a lion.

Unfortunately for Boone, he would be unable to fill even the meager capacity afforded by the Plaza de Toros arena. Most newspapers in Mexico and the United States refused to publish news of the fight, believing that something so ridiculous must be a joke. It did not help that Boone scheduled the bout for April 1, April Fools' Day. Also, it seems that Boone kept ticket prices similar to what they had been in San Francisco. Whereas the wealthy merchants of San Francisco could shell out twenty dollars for a trivial event, the people of poverty-stricken Mexico and South Texas had no such disposable income. There would be plenty of empty seats for the showdown between Ramadan and Parnell.

When Boone's long-planned event finally took place on April 1, 1895, it was in front of a sparse but eclectic crowd of Mexican politicians, businessmen from the United States and a handful of ranchers that had scrounged up enough money to pay for the costly tickets. A few workers selling confectioneries, attendants working the show and some poor locals who snuck into the event were also in attendance. The only reporter seems to have been a Mr. Zercombe, the editor from the local Laredo newspaper who decided to take his camera to photograph the bout. Newspapers would later feature versions of Zercombe's account of the battle.

Economic and national background faded away when Parnell was wheeled into the arena, the lion having been kept outside the stadium until the fight began. Ramadan was in the center of the bullring in the fight cage, isolated from the crowd by a canvas covering. The draping was removed only after Parnell's transportable cage was placed beside Ramadan's. The two animals reacted excitedly upon seeing each other. They were scared by the noises and mass of humanity and were prepared to fight. As one observer noted, "Everything was in striking contrast, it seemed to me, but brute and humanity."[10]

Ramadan sat on his hind legs opposite the cage from the entryway. When an attendant opened the door separating the two animals, Parnell sprang into action. Leaping fifteen feet into the air, the lion spanned the length of the cage and came down on Ramadan. The grizzly, however, managed to stand on his hind legs and extend his forepaws to stop the lion before he could sink his teeth into its throat. The two animals held this upright grappling position, Parnell scratching and clawing at Ramadan's thick hide, while the grizzly did his best to hold off the lion's bite. The bear was unable to do any damage to his opponent, while the cat successfully used its claws to rip chunks of flesh from Ramadan's underbelly. One observer noted that the animal "seemed bent on carpeting the cage with fur."[11] If not for the

STANDING UPRIGHT BOTH, ANIMALS TRIED FOR THE "BACK HOLD."
[From an instantaneous photograph taken by Zercombe of Laredo.]

Artist depiction of Ramadan and Parnell's cage fight. As often happens in fight sports during perceived lulls in action, the audience booed when the bear and lion held on to each other for nineteen minutes. *From the* San Francisco Examiner, *April 7, 1895.*

bear's thick hide, Parnell would likely have released Ramadan's internal organs, putting a quick end to the fight. Finally, after nineteen minutes, the combatants fell to the ground.

Parnell sat up and began sniping at Ramadan, the grizzly unable to bring his claws or teeth to bare on the lion. Every time the bruin lunged at the African cat, the more agile lion simply sidestepped and swiped at his opponent. When Parnell came in for one of his strikes, the bear stood on his hind legs and once again grappled the lion. This time, however, Parnell got past the bear's forepaws and sunk his teeth into the animal's neck. Ramadan responded by using his brute strength to hug the lion. Shocked by the pressure, Parnell let loose his bite, allowing the grizzly to toss and then mount his opponent. Although Parnell escaped before the bear could do any damage, Ramadan had clearly found a way to defend himself.

The two animals circled each other in the cage before Parnell once again pounced and sank his teeth into Ramadan's neck. Again the bear responded by hugging his opponent with all his might. The lion's teeth sank deeper.

In response, the grizzly's grip grew tighter. To those in attendance, it was unclear which of the beasts would give in first. Then, without warning, the lion let go and bellowed out a roar of pain, the bear's hold so tight that one observer remarked, "I could almost hear the bones cracking." Ramadan then grabbed Parnell with "a beautiful half Nelson that would have done credit to a professional wrestler" and hurled the lion.[12]

Parnell turned a complete somersault in the air before landing on his feet in the center of the cage. Recovering quickly, the lion drew its claws across Ramadan's neck and then circled and attacked the bruin from the rear. The bear, showing agility not seen up to this point, turned, grabbed the lion and lifted him into the air. With Parnell's head dangling, Ramadan began squeezing and shaking the feline as if it weighed the same as a house cat. Ramadan then lifted his opponent into the air and threw him against the side of the cage.

Parnell's head struck a steel bar with a thud, and the lion collapsed to the ground. He remained unconscious for more than a minute before slowly getting to his feet. Although the lion again attempted to attack Ramadan, it was clear that he had little fight left in him. He was slow and struggled to walk. Ramadan also appeared to be done fighting, choosing to parade around the cage instead of continuing the battle. After thirty-three total minutes in the cage, Parnell collapsed to the ground and refused to get up. He was exhausted and possibly suffering from broken ribs and internal bleeding. The fight was over.

The crowd, promised a fight to the death by Boone's advertisements, started booing. Although they had just witnessed an epic encounter in which both animals put up a spectacular fight, the multitude wanted blood. Under pressure from the crowd, ringside attendants attempted to restart the fight by prodding Parnell with metal poles and hot irons. The African cat, however, had had enough. He was done. No amount of cajoling would get him to take on that grizzly again.

Denied the death that they had grown to expect from years of watching bullfights, the Mexicans in the audience began jeering and throwing things at Boone, demanding their money back in a flurry of Spanish epithets. Fearing that a riot would break out, Mexican police placed Boone under arrest for false advertising. They escorted the showman out of the arena, placed him in the local jail and demanded that Boone refund the crowd's money before they would release him. It appears that the lion tamer complied with the request, meaning that for all his efforts, Boone made no money. Not only that, but the main purpose of the fight had been to put

THE LION RECOVERING FROM A TERRIFIC BLOW DELIVERED BY THE GRIZZLY.
[From an instantaneous photograph taken by Zercombe of Laredo.]

The lion-bear fight ended after Parnell collapsed and Ramadan refused to fight any longer. *From the* San Francisco Examiner, *April 7, 1895.*

down Parnell, and although injured, the resolute animal still held on to life and appeared to be recovering.

E. Daniel Boone had put on a battle never before seen in world history. The show, however, did not have the effect that he intended. The audience that witnessed an American grizzly fight an African lion had no appreciation for what they were watching; not only had Boone failed to profit, but he also still had the same problematic lion that he had when he came to Mexico. Indeed, rumors traveled throughout Laredo that Boone committed suicide in the fight's aftermath. He had not. Instead, the situation convinced the vaudevillian that the only solution to his financial and logistical woes was to stage additional interspecies fights.

CHAPTER 2

THE LION, THE BEAR AND THE BULL (PART II)

Newspapers throughout the United States reported on Parnell and Ramadan's epic bout. Many carried some version of Laredo journalist Zercombe's account of what happened. Others took rumors and concocted details to fill in missing parts of the story. Most of the various articles reported that the grizzly Ramadan had been the victor, while others said that because neither animal died, the bout was a draw. None of the articles carried a photograph, as few newspapers of the time could mass-produce photograph prints. However, the William Randolph Hearst–owned *San Francisco Examiner* purchased at least three of Zercombe's photographs and had its artist reproduce what they depicted in a format that the newspaper could carry. Whether because of the artist's skill or the technological limitations of printing presses of the time, these depictions had few details.

The ambiguity in reporting and the dearth of details created a sense of mystery to Ramadan and Parnell's fight, and people throughout the United States demanded to know more. Boone was determined to capitalize on the notoriety. Shortly after the fight, he announced that Ramadan would face a Mexican bull named Panthera from the famous Las Cruces Ranch. It is unclear why Boone decided to pit Ramadan against this specific animal, but it would not be hard to imagine that a local offered up the animal as an opponent for the bear and Boone, seeing a chance to recoup his money, accepted the challenge.

A SPECIMEN OF THE LION'S INFIGHTING WITH JAWS AND CLAWS JUST BEFORE HE WAS HURLED INTO THE AIR BY THE GRIZZLY.
[From an instantaneous photograph taken by Zercombe of Laredo.]

Artist sketch of Parnell and Ramadan's bout as featured in the *Examiner*. *From the* San Francisco Examiner, *April 7, 1895.*

A product of hundreds of years of selective breeding, Panthera was essentially a human creation. He was massive, weighing more than half a ton, much heavier than cattle in the wild. Panthera was also more aggressive than other cattle. His ancestors had been used to fight humans, rhinos, elephants and other animal combatants in the Roman coliseum. The Spanish had later chosen the most violent and successful of these bulls to breed, and over time they created animals like Panthera, whose main purpose was to bring harm. And Panthera could bring harm, especially with the long, sharp horns that protruded from his skull. One witness called him "a powerful brute from the southern mesas and as pugnacious as a badger."[13]

Panthera's massive size meant that Ramadan would be giving up the weight advantage he had held in his fight with Parnell. He would also have to adjust to a different cage size, as the cage's diameter was increased from twenty to thirty feet to allow the bull more room to maneuver. Ramadan still held several advantages over Panthera, particularly when it came to close combat, as he had more weapons than his bovine opponent. Whereas the bull had only his horns and head, the bear sported four claws and a vicious set of teeth.

Boone set the bout between Ramadan and Panthera to take place at 3:30 p.m. on April 14 and made great efforts to advertise the event. Newspapers speculated on who would win, and reports show the fight taking on nationalistic overtones in the two weeks leading up to the event. Hearst's *San Francisco Examiner* sent its own photographer, even though the newspaper lacked the ability to print photos, and others showed up hoping to sell their photos to other periodicals. Those on the United States side of the border backed the American grizzly, while Mexicans favored the home-grown Panthera. The nationalism fueled ticket sales, and the event sold out quickly, with approximately half of the 650 available seats going to persons from Mexico and half to those from the United States. Gamblers also fell prey to the nationalistic overtones, with bets on the winner as large as $100.

When fight time came and attendees brought Panthera into the ring, it was obvious that the bull was ready for a fight. Its tail lashed in the air, and it lunged any time someone got close to the cage. This included the numerous photographers who had showed up in the hopes of selling their photos. The constant ignition of their flash powder especially irked Panthera, and on more than one occasion, the bull bent the cage's bars in an attempt to ram a photographer.

The assault on the cage continued when Ramadan was wheeled into the arena at 4:45 p.m. and was met with enormous cheers from the Americans among the crowd. As the bear came closer, Panthera began ramming his cage in anticipation of the fight ahead. Indeed, Panthera was so agitated that in order to allow Ramadan a safe entry into the cage, it was necessary for a bullfighter to go to the opposite end of the arena and wave a flag to distract the bull. With Panthera occupied, attendants opened Ramadan's cage, and the bear headed in the direction of his opponent.

When the bullfighter backed away from the cage, Panthera turned to find that a strange, hairy creature was heading in his direction. Before the bear could close any more distance, the bull lowered its head and ran directly at his opponent. Likely never having seen an animal this large, nevertheless one heading straight for him, Ramadan grew confused and turned to one side, opening himself up to a direct charge.

This allowed Panthera to drive one of his horns full speed into Ramadan's shoulder, goring the bear. Ramadan howled in pain. Confused and unable to grab the bull as he had done with Parnell two weeks before, Ramadan began running in circles around the cage. Panthera pursued until he backed Ramadan against the bars, trapping his opponent. When the bull went in for a second charge, Ramadan swiped viciously and "ripped a great chunk of flesh off the bull's neck," managing to drive the bull back temporarily.[14] The bear then used the opportunity to retreat to the other side of cage, but he was confused and hurt and did not want to fight anymore. He wanted out.

To the shock of everyone in attendance, Ramadan wrapped his claws around the cage bars and started climbing to freedom. In an instant, the bear scaled the fifteen-foot cage, which had no top to it, and prepared to jump into the open arena. The sight of a bleeding, angry bear sent the crowd running for the exits. People who had not exercised since childhood found themselves on their feet, trying to push their way to safety. Those in the top rows of the bullring prepared to leap the twenty-five feet to the ground outside of the arena. Fortunately for them—one newspaper speculated that the bear did not want anyone to lose their life in the scramble—Ramadan abandoned his escape plan and lowered himself back into the cage with Panthera.

The climb and the loss of blood from Panthera's first charge took its toll on Ramadan. He sat on his haunches and refused to fight. The bull, likewise, did not seem interested in opening himself up to another bear attack and was content with pacing on its side of the cage. Unwilling to call the fight so soon, either Boone or the arena owners had a bullfighter position himself behind Ramadan and wave a red flag to draw Panthera's ire. It worked, and the bull charged. Ramadan saw his opponent's approach and attempted to raise himself up for an attack. He was too slow. Panthera drove his horns directly into Ramadan's side. The bear responded by swiping his claws across the bull's head and retreating to the other side of the cage.

When Panthera once again approached, Ramadan was ready. He reared up and clawed the bull about the neck and head. The grizzly then went to bite the bull's jugular. Unfortunately for the bear, Panthera was raising his head at the moment of attack, and one of the bull's horns pierced the bear through the cheek. Blood flowed from Ramadan's mouth as Panthera

Panthera's repeated charges led Ramadan to try to climb out of the cage. *From the* St. Louis Post Dispatch, *May 5, 1895.*

THE FIGHT BETWEEN THE BULL AND THE GRIZZLY BEAR AT LA-REDO, TEX.

withdrew his horn. Pressing his advantage, Panthera charged the injured bear, ramming him so hard that Ramadan's feet left the ground.

Ramadan could not mount a comeback. He lay there while Panthera took potshots at him. Wanting to avoid the inconclusive end of the previous fight, trainers prodded the grizzly until he half-heartedly went after the bull. The attacks had no force behind them, and the exertion did little more than speed up Ramadan's blood loss. The bruin labored around the ring, breathing heavily, until after almost an hour of constant punishment, the mighty grizzly put his head on the ground, closed his eyes and died.

Although some among the crowd complained that the bout was lacking in action when compared to the lion-bear fight, most left satisfied, and with Ramadan's death, no one had a reason to demand their money back. Boone had finally made money off an animal cage fighting event, but it seems that with the revenue lost in the previous event, he was still in the hole financially. Fortunately for the promoter, newspapers throughout the United States once again reported the events on the border, eliciting a demand for additional bouts. Therefore, in a last-ditch effort to recoup his loses, Boone scheduled a third bout. Parnell would take on Panthera the following week, completing the king of the beasts' trifecta.

Boone initially contemplated replacing Parnell with another lion from his menagerie, fearing that the feline had yet to recover from his fight with Ramadan two weeks before. Therefore, to test Parnell's fighting capability, Boone put a goat in his cage. Parnell, showing no signs that a grizzly had recently tossed him around a steel ring, leaped on the goat, tore it to shreds, and ate it. A few days later, Boone put in a young steer, only for the lion to tear open its throat and make it a meal.

It was apparent that Parnell was still vicious, something that George Rooke, a trainer who had accompanied Boone on his trip to Nuevo Laredo, found out the hard way. Shortly before the scheduled fight with Panthera, Rooke stood too close to Parnell's cage. With no warning, the lion leaped forward, grabbed Rooke by the arm and dragged him against the cage, trapping the trainer's shoulders between two bars. Unable to get free of Parnell's grip, Rooke screamed and then fainted. Meeting no resistance, Parnell used his teeth to rip the man's bicep from his arm. His follow-up bite broke bone. The lion let up only after those around the cage began beating him about the face with crowbars.

Boone immediately took Rooke, "his arm hanging on by only tendon and flesh" and "chewed to shreds," to a nearby hospital.[15] The severity of the injury forced the doctors to amputate the trainer's arm. Likely owing to the unsanitary conditions in the 1890s, there were complications with the surgery, and Rooke developed something that newspapers called "blood poisoning."[16] The trainer was unable to fend off the bacterial infection, or whatever had inflicted him, and he died shortly thereafter. Parnell's human body count was up to two.

News of Parnell's vicious attack, nationalistic enthusiasm for the Mexican bull Panthera and advertisements Boone placed in newspapers in the United States and Mexico created an even greater demand for a third fight. Realizing that he could sell more tickets if he moved to a larger venue, Boone rented a bullring one hundred miles south of the border in Monterrey, Mexico. The new arena had two thousand seats, all of which sold out for the upcoming fight.

When the fight day arrived on April 21, Panthera once again appeared ready for battle, showing no sign that the injuries sustained in his fight with Ramadan would affect his performance in the cage. As the bull paraded about the arena, the mostly Mexican crowd cheered their champion and met Parnell's entrance with boos.

The fight started in much the same way as Panthera and Ramadan's bout. The bull charged the lion, intending to gore it, as he had done with the bear. But Parnell was much quicker than Ramadan. He quickly moved out of the way of Panthera's horns. The bull continued to charge, but Parnell was too fast, avoiding the larger animal whenever he approached. The lion even went on the offensive, swiping at the bovine's snout whenever the bull came near. One blow opened a gash in Panthera's nose, and blood began pouring out. The wound was made worse when the bull scraped his snout against the ground to get low enough to eviscerate Parnell with his horns.

When Panthera charged again, Parnell leaped into the air and came down on the bull's neck. The bull lacked the thick hide that had protected Ramadan, so Parnell's teeth sank deep, opening an artery and sending blood streaming down Panthera's body. The lion held on to his grip for twenty-four minutes, as the bull jerked his head and jabbed its front feet on its attacker to shake it loose but failed. Although the bull managed to free himself by stepping on Parnell's legs, Parnell quickly bit Panthera's snout, and "the sound of the cracking and breaking of the bull's nasal and upper jaw bones could be heard all over the amphitheater."[17] It looked like the lion was about to take down an animal twice his size.

However, instead of capitalizing on Panthera's injuries, Parnell released his bite and went to the edge of the cage and lowered himself against it. In one sense, the move was smart, as the lion made himself a small target. He

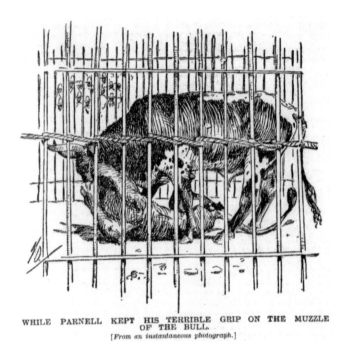

WHILE PARNELL KEPT HIS TERRIBLE GRIP ON THE MUZZLE OF THE BULL.
[From an instantaneous photograph.]

Newspaper reports of the fights on the border often anthropomorphized animals and assigned complex motivations or emotions to explain their actions in the cage. The *Examiner* portrayed Parnell's decision to stay low as a strategy to avoid Panthera's horns, while the *Times* called the lion "cowardly." *From the* San Francisco Examiner, *May 1, 1895.*

was situated so close to the cage that Panthera would fear rushing him from the side, lest he tangle his horns in the steel bars. If the bull attempted to hit Parnell directly, the lion's proximity to the ground meant there was a good chance the bull would miss and hit his head on the side of the cage. No matter what Panthera did, Parnell would be in a good position to capitalize on his opponent's mistake.

Parnell did not consider that the bloodthirsty crowd would refuse to accept a temporary reprieve in action. After Panthera attempted to lower himself enough to attack Parnell and failed, both animals stopped fighting, leading the spectators to hiss and boo. Following several minutes with no action, one of the venue's owners decided to push the action by forcing Parnell to leave the safety of the edge of the cage. A vaquero reached through the bars and strung a noose around Parnell's neck. The cowboy then threaded the rope to the other side of the cage and pulled, dragging the lion to the center of the arena. Parnell, lacking oxygen from the assault and unable to move with the rope around his neck, was defenseless.

Now that his opponent was safely away from the steel bars, Panthera backed up and charged. Because Parnell was unable to move, the bull did not have to readjust his aim, allowing all his momentum to come down on the lion. The blow was devastating. The lion crumpled into a ball, flew to the top of the cage and came down in a heap. Panthera did not give up, continuing to gore the downed Parnell. With one devastating blow, the bull drove a horn through the lion's shoulder. Panthera then lifted his massive head, with Parnell still dangling from his horn, and marched proudly around the arena. Only after the jungle cat ceased moving did Boone call an end to the fight, at which point "the bull gave a final toss of his head, and the lion dropped limp and lifeless to the ground."[18] Boone had finally managed to euthanize his man-killing lion.

Mexican attendees in the crowd cried out "Viva México!" and "otro león!"[19] Their champion Panthera had defeated both animals put against him, making a considerable amount of money for those who had bet on him and serving as a temporary hero to the people of Mexico. Unfortunately, it is unclear if Panthera was able to capitalize on his newfound fame, as one newspaper reported that the bull lost too much blood and died soon after the match. Another, however, held that the animal survived his wounds. If so, it would not be hard to imagine Panthera living out the rest of his life as a breeding bull.

Panthera carries Parnell's lifeless body around the ring. Accounts differ over specifics of the fight, with one version saying that Parnell survived long enough to crawl back to his cage. *From* The Inquirer, *February 12, 1905.*

Although the Mexicans in the crowd were happy, it seems that Boone was not, as he had reportedly bet a significant amount of money on Parnell to win. So much that apparently the financial loss offset the money he had made in ticket sales, meaning that despite his efforts, he would be leaving Mexico poorer than he had arrived. One report held that Boone grew depressed and even contemplated suicide not only because of his financial situation, but also because after the third fight, he finally felt empathy for his animals. According to one report, when Parnell closed his eyes for the last time, Boone apparently concluded "that he was a murderer and deserved to die."[20]

If Boone were depressed after throwing away the lives of two or three majestic animals for the entertainment of unappreciative, bloodthirsty audiences, the feeling was short-lived. Indeed, one newspaper reported that he returned to Mexico in 1898 to again fight a lion against a bull. The lion was apparently not as vicious as Parnell and put up such a weak fight that a local governor ordered Boone to refund everyone's money.

Boone continued to train animals after he returned from Mexico, and it seems that he recovered from his financial instability. He made enough from his shows to add a monkey; Holy Moses, a two-humped camel; and a "sociable pig" to his cadre of animals.[21] He also introduced new acts, including Hootchie Cootchie, a bear who drank booze, and Bob Fitzsimmons, a boxing kangaroo. Boone still had trouble with his lions. Two of the animals killed another trainer, and third lion escaped its cage while Boone was touring in Memphis.

Perhaps owing to the headaches caused by such instances, by 1901 Boone had grown weary of the circus business. He attempted to find work as a zookeeper in Washington, D.C., but it seems that no reputable organization wanted to hire him. With few options, Boone sold his animals and retired to San Francisco, where he died in 1903.

CHAPTER 3

BILLY VERSUS THE BULL

T he United States–Mexico border would not see another series of fights on the scale of the Parnell-Ramadan-Panthera bouts over the next decade, but bullrings on the border, and particularly the Ciudad Juárez bullring, would be home to a variety of unusual spectacles, including multiple interspecies cage fights. The people who put on these fights were an eccentric lot and included a Spanish bullfighter who hoped to broaden the appeal of his sport to an American audience, a lion tamer who was willing to sacrifice his friend to win a few dollars and an African American man who fought bulls and bears and claimed to be the boxing and wrestling champion of Mexico and South America. The reactions to these events varied, but in more than one instance, riots erupted; one promoter lost his life after a failed event. These post-fight spectacles often overshadowed what went on in the cage.

The events on the border at the turn of the twentieth century also reflected larger trends in Mexico, the United States and the world at large, and they serve to tell a history of the time. This was the case with the story of Billy Clarke (also spelled "Clark"), an African American boxer who traveled to Mexico in 1894 in the hopes of earning a living as a fighter. The 1890s was a bad time to be a boxer of African ancestry in the United States. Prior to 1865, owing to slavery in the South, racism and poverty in the North and the fact that professional sports were uncommon anywhere in the United States, few people of color played sports. Following the Civil War and spurred on by the reformist politics of Reconstruction, African American participation in sports increased. Black jockeys won the Kentucky Derby multiple times, and numerous African Americans competed against whites in professional baseball. Black boxers also often fought white fighters, with African American George Dixon winning the bantamweight title in 1890.

This brief period of partial integration came to an end in the late nineteenth century when white southern Democrats regained control of state and federal offices in the South and passed Jim Crow laws segregating government facilities. Private businesses and venues also segregated, banning African Americans from performing in venues throughout the South. This hurt revenue, caused issues with integrated sports that operated in both the North and South and led several white sportsmen to refuse to play against people of color. To appease southern audiences, white promoters in professional baseball made a "gentleman's agreement" to exclude players of African ancestry.

Boxing remained integrated longer than other sports in the United States, and officially it would never become segregated. However, at the turn of the twentieth century, many white boxers began "drawing the color line" and refusing to fight African American opponents. Black boxers often struggled to secure quality bouts because while white fighters might box opponents of color on their way to a championship, they often refused to cross racial lines once they had earned a title. Considering ubiquitous economic inequalities within the United States and that many whites preferred to see fighters of their own race, African American boxers found it much more difficult to earn a living than white boxers of equivalent skill.

Billy Clarke was an African American fighter who hoped to avoid this racism by seeking out opponents in Latin America. Little is known of Clarke's upbringing except that he was born in Philadelphia around 1870. At some point in his youth, he took up both boxing and wrestling, and although Clarke appears to have dedicated himself to these fight sports, he was not particularly skilled. He often overexerted himself and had a hard time avoiding punches. He made up for this lack of finesse with extensive practice, which allowed him to develop sound technique and learn enough about boxing to teach others, earning himself the nickname "Professor." However, Clarke's greatest asset in the ring was his strength, developed through weightlifting and resistance training. By the time he was an adult, Clarke had developed an impressive physique. Although only five-foot-nine, he entered the ring at more than 180 pounds.

Clarke would later claim to have spent his early twenties traveling throughout Central and South America, earning multiple boxing and

Billy Clarke demonstrating a contemporary boxing stance. Boxing gloves of the time had little padding, meaning that fighters were more likely to break their hands if they adopted a modern stance and tried to block punches with the back of their hands. *From* El Paso Herald, *July 19, 1900.*

wrestling championships and amassing an undefeated record. It is difficult to prove the veracity of these claims, with one newspaper noting that "his record is but slightly known," but Clarke did box and teach boxing in Guatemala.[22] Historian David C. LaFevor suspects that Clarke arrived in Central America with other Americans to work on the railroads, took fights in his spare time and did well in them, leading Clarke to pursue boxing as a full-time profession.

Although little more is known about Clarke's early career, he understood that his race meant limited opportunities and competition if he returned to the United States, so he traveled to Mexico in 1894. Once there, he found that while there were no race restrictions in Mexico, there were also no boxers. With little historical or cultural precedence, few Mexicans had interest in the sport. The president of Mexico, Porfirio Díaz, had also recently spoken out against prizefighting, and although he had left it to the states to determine its legality, he hinted that a federal ban on boxing may be forthcoming.

Fortunately for Clarke, Mexico had a substantial American expatriate community that enjoyed boxing and was willing to test the law to watch it. In 1895, Clarke or his manager gained special permission from the governor of Hidalgo to hold a gloved heavyweight, three-minutes-per-round bout in the city of Pachuca. Pachuca made a good location for the fight. It was only a short train ride from Mexico City, where most American expats lived, but far enough away from the capital to avoid federal oversight. Indeed, thrill-seekers often made their way from Mexico City to Hidalgo to gamble and partake in other activities restricted by the Mexican government. Unfortunately, Hidalgo lacked an indoor venue capable of hosting the fight, so promoters rented out a local bullring.

Clarke's opponent in his first match in Mexico would be Billy Smith, a white Australian who had earned the title "Champion of Texas" after an impressive boxing career in El Paso. The Texas government had recently banned prizefighting, as had the federal government in the neighboring New Mexico Territory, forcing Smith to relocate to Mexico, where he agreed to fight Clarke. The winner of the bout would receive a $2,000 purse and a pig.

On the day of the fight, November 24, 1895, a crowd of eight hundred mostly American spectators took the train from Mexico City to Hidalgo to witness the event. When the fight began, Clarke came out strong, landing multiple devastating blows in the first round. Unfortunately, it seems that his stamina ran out quickly—likely owing to a buildup of lactic acid created by his substantial muscle mass—and Clarke found it hard to defend against his opponent's attacks. This allowed Smith to pepper Clarke with quick jabs and crosses throughout the second, and by the third, Smith had "turned Clark into a punching bag."[23] Clarke dropped to the canvas in the fourth, and although he managed to avoid a ten count and stagger back to his corner, he fell unconscious and was unable to return for a fifth round, awarding Smith the victory.

The fight received both positive and negative attention in the Mexican press, with the consensus of newspapers expressing curiosity about boxing but lacking the vocabulary and pugilistic knowledge to properly explain what exactly had taken place. *El Diario del Hogar*, for example, broke down the fight by explaining that the fighters unleashed *golpes* to one another's faces and stomachs, with Clarke losing simply because he received more than Smith. A report in *El Siglo Diez y Nueve* carried a more in-depth analysis, although it, too, simplified the victory to Smith hitting Clarke in the mouth more than the other way around.

Other newspapers in Mexico chose to focus on the sensational aspects of the fight and its aftermath. *El Correo Español*, for example, contained elaborate descriptions of the fighters' dress and focused on the controversy Clarke generated afterward by claiming that the fight was rigged. His loss was only because the referee favored Smith and failed to call a clear "below the belt" shot. Clarke also blamed his corner man for dropping the water he used to sponge off between rounds and replacing it with iced tea with lemon, which, according to Clarke, made his body feel "spongy."[24] Newspapers also reported on the fact that Smith's new pig jumped to its death from his hotel balcony after the fight, supposedly to avoid getting beaten as badly as Clarke had been.

Other Mexican periodicals responded to the boxing match with revulsion. Mexican artist José Guadalupe Posada, famed for his macabre drawings of skeletons performing human actions, drew an image of the fight with Smith backing Clarke to the edge of ring. Posada's frequent character Don Chepito Marihuano—a middle-class, marijuana-smoking, wannabe member of the bourgeois—cheers from a railing to show that he is just as cultured as the Americans who enjoy boxing. The newspaper *Voz de México* was more straightforward in commenting "it is incredible that a civilized country would permit such a repugnant spectacle" and called on the government to ban boxing in the future.[25]

President Díaz agreed, admonished the governor of Hidalgo for allowing the bout, and banned boxing at the federal level. Participants in future matches faced arrest. Unable to continue his craft in Mexico and with boxing banned in Texas and New Mexico, Smith returned to El Paso, started an athletic club and joined the city police force. In February 1896, heavyweight boxers Bob Fitzsimmons and Peter Maher tested Mexico and Texas's bans by holding a fight on a sandbar in the middle of the Rio Grande. Although they carried out the fight without disruption, the remote location and clandestine nature of the event limited attendance, and after both men returned to the United States, no one repeated the stunt.

With Smith, Fitzsimmons, and Maher gone, this left Clarke as the only boxer to have legally competed in Mexico. Clarke took this to mean that he was now the official "Champion of Mexico." One newspaper reported that Clarke was able to adopt the title because "nobody else claimed it" and noted that from that time forward, Clarke "claims to be a general champion of just about everything in Mexico."[26] Unable to legally fight but hoping to make a living off boxing and his new title, Clarke opened the Olympic Club of Mexico, an athletic venue in Mexico City that could house 1,200 people when at capacity.

José Guadalupe Posada's drawing of Clarke and Smith's bout. Don Chepito Marihuano sits on the bullring fence pretending to enjoy the fight to impress the Americans in attendance. *Metropolitan Museum of Art.*

Declaring himself to be a "physical culture professor"[27] and a "professor of pugilism,"[28] Clarke trained prospective fighters and those who could afford his classes. Multiple Mexican boxers trained with Clarke. He also held parties at the Olympic Club, where he put on feats of strength and other entertainment. The biggest draw to the parties, and one that would get him into trouble more than anything else, were the underground boxing matches. Clarke, like many boxers in areas of the United States where boxing was banned, realized that if he couched a competitive match as a non-competitive boxing "exhibition" meant to educate the public on the art of boxing, it would draw crowds without technically violating the law. Therefore, Clarke began putting on "plays" and "scientific shows" that were really boxing matches, bringing hundreds to his club on fight nights.[29] He profited by charging entrance fees, holding raffles and selling alcohol and memorabilia.

The entertainment at the Olympic Club ran afoul of Mexican law, and the police arrested Clarke on multiple occasions. Charges included raffling a life-size picture of himself without a license and selling alcohol without a license, the latter netting a sixty-six-dollar fine. The illegal boxing matches caused Clarke the most problems. In 1896, Mexican authorities threw him in Belém Prison for prizefighting after a bout against Ben Chapman. Clarke tried to argue that "it was all a farce," to no avail.[30] In 1897, the governor of the Distrito Federal warned Clarke that he would expel him from the country "the next time he attempts to conduct a prize fight under the guise of a scientific boxing experiment."[31]

Faced with prison time and exile, Clarke tried to go legit and put on a variety show at his athletic club, calling himself and his performers the Billy Clarke Variety Company.[32] He did magic and acrobatics and performed feats of strength. In the first performance, Clarke demonstrated his muscularity by standing on a Persian rug and posing like Greek and Roman statues. He also reenacted historical scenes such as Brutus looking down on Caesar after stabbing him. He would change outfits throughout the show, at one point wearing General Wolfe's hat and posing as the general had when he lay dying following the Battle of Quebec. Clarke then dared everyone in the audience to challenge him to tug of war. No one took him up on the offer.

While newspapers lauded the performance, few went to the show. He started opening night performing in front of ten people, and another show netted only fifteen dollars. This led Clarke to determine that he was unappreciated. He derided the fact that audiences wanted to see him fight and perform feats of strength, not theater. The lack of audience for his artistic endeavors and the police pressure on his boxing eventually forced Clarke to shut down the athletic club in Mexico City and open another in Puebla, where there was less scrutiny and the laws regarding physical sports were more lax. Unfortunately for Clark, it seems that the police in Puebla were also unwilling to sanction boxing matches.

With the police cracking down and his attempts to turn legit failing, Clarke began staging wrestling matches at his new club. Wrestling occupied more of a legal gray area than boxing, in part because it had some preexisting cultural appeal. During France's brief occupation of Mexico in the 1860s, French soldiers staged wrestling tournaments and taught the Greco-Roman style to curious Mexicans. By the 1890s, Mexico had become home to a few, mostly European wrestlers who put on exhibitions throughout the nation.

Clarke adopted the name the "Colored Hercules" and traveled throughout Mexico, calling out local wrestlers in newspapers and putting up his "Champion of Mexico" title to anyone who could beat him. If a wrestler refused, Clarke would claim that the fighter "was afraid of him" in an attempt to drum up sales and goad the fighter into a matchup.[33] If they accepted a bout and could agree to terms, Clarke would plaster life-size images of himself throughout town to advertise the fight and find a local promoter to place a bet on himself. If Clarke won, he stood to make money off ticket sales and his bet. If he lost, he could recoup expenses by saying that the match was rigged and demanding a rematch.

From what little information is available, Clarke sometimes dominated opponents and other times backed down when it appeared that he would lose. For example, in 1897, he challenged Sicilian strongman Romulus to a wrestling match in the Bucareli bullring, saying that the Italian was ducking him. Romulus responded by saying that he would fight if Clarke was willing to put up $2,000 against his $2,000, with winner taking all. Romulus wanted to name the judges and have the first person to pin the other be declared the winner. Clarke refused these conditions, and the two went back and forth in the press. Eventually, the two combatants met in a match that was drawn by José Guadalupe Posada, with Clarke emerging victorious. However, in 1899, Clarke faced a humiliating defeat to French wrestler Louis Planchette.

At least one historian put Clarke among a group of late nineteenth- and early twentieth-century wrestlers in Mexico who laid the foundations for modern *lucha libre*. In addition to wrestling, *lucha libre* fighters adopt a simplistic identity and build drama in the lead-up to fights to sell tickets. In the late 1800s, Romulus was the intimidating Italian strongman, while Clarke was the showy, audacious African American who was stronger than his competitors but lacked finesse. Newspapers of the time sometimes even portrayed him as little more than bumbling simpleton, a deviation of the Sambo character that was popular in Mexico at the time. Of course, the fact that Clarke ran an athletic club, performed magic shows and acted in plays while competing in wrestling shows that he was highly intelligent and complex, but *lucha libre* fans were not interested in complexity, so Clarke played into stereotypes.

Many in Mexico welcomed the eccentric American showman and his routine. The editor of the English-language *Mexican Herald*, for example, devoted numerous front-page articles to Clarke's exploits. Opinion pieces in the newspaper called the fighter a "genius" entertainer, and on more than one occasion, Billy wrote to the *Herald* to explain his latest ventures.[34] The praise levied by the *Herald* was often paternalistic and tongue-in-cheek, but it seems that the paper genuinely had the fighter's best interests at heart. For example, when the editor of *El Tráfico*, published in Guaymas, bad-mouthed Clarke and expressed his fears that the American would "get spoiled and wind up marrying an Indian girl and flood the country with an undesirable race of hybrids," the editor of the *Herald* gleefully pointed out that Clarke had already married a Mexican woman and the couple had multiple children.[35]

Unfortunately, while wrestling earned him a degree of fame, it was not an answer to Clarke's financial woes. It was difficult to acquire permits for events, as many Mexican authorities classified wrestling as a form of prizefighting. It was also tough to find opponents of equal caliber. The fact that wrestling had only recently became popular in Mexico meant that local opponents were usually little challenge, while the only outsiders were professionals from Europe, such as the Frenchman Planchette, with much more experience who could easily defeat Clarke in unrigged fights.

This lack of competition and a desire for money led Clarke to fight animals. It is unclear when he first engaged in the practice, but the fights became frequent in the late 1890s. According to one report, Clarke fought a lion, although little is known of the bout. Colonel Robert Pate, whom one newspaper called "our modern Roman, who is ready to give us gladiatorial shows," advertised that he planned to put Billy and a bear in a cage at his Indianilla racetrack in Mexico City.[36] Perhaps viewing the exhibition as akin to bullfighting, the Mexican government determined that a man fighting a bear was less objectionable than a man fighting a man and allowed the exhibition to proceed.

In 1898, Clarke purchased a bear, which he fought at his athletic club in Puebla and brought on tour with him throughout Mexico. The animal was muzzled and its claws trimmed, but it still fought Clarke with ferocity, and their fights became both legendary and infamous in Mexico. In one, Clarke defeated the bear, "holding it tightly in his grip and preventing its moving."[37] This delighted the audience. They demanded an immediate rematch, and Clarke once again emerged the victor.

Clarke was not always victorious in his fights with bruins. In a fight against a bear in Puebla, the bear managed to pin Clarke to the ground and was set to maul him until a trainer clubbed the animal over the head, allowing Clarke to claim that he won the match. In another match in Pachuca, a bear "handled Billy so roughly" that after the match, Clarke grew angry and punched a fellow wrestler in the heart, sending the man to the hospital.[38] Instead of apologizing or paying for the wrestler's hospital bills, Clarke supposedly stole the injured man's cannonballs and turned them into dumbbells for his strongman show.

The poor exhibitions may have owed to Clarke's increasingly self-destructive behavior. As his popularity in Mexico increased, he began to eat and drink too much. When first arriving in Mexico, Clarke claimed, "I never either smoke, or drink any stimulants."[39] While that might have been true at one point, within a few years, Clarke was not only smoking but also served as a spokesman for the La Flor de Cuba cigarette brand, with the company claiming that the "strong and robust" boxer "knew how to live."[40]

Clarke also drank booze, or at least he did by 1898. One report held that the pugilist would imbibe "copious libations of tequila" before fights, which "screwed up his courage" but caused him to perform poorly.[41] Clarke also seems to have eaten badly, engaged in late-night festivities and possibly conducted extra-marital affairs. After one fight with a bear, "he went to a restaurant followed by a servant girl bearing a platter on which was a dead cat which Billy presented to the cook with the request that pussy be nicely stewed à vafricaine."[42] The chef declined to cook the unusual dish. Clarke also gambled heavily. By 1899, he had supposedly saved $20,000 from a recent round of fights, and he planned to use the money to move to Kansas City and open a boxing gym. Unfortunately, he gambled and lost all the money, which one newspaper incorrectly reported led him to commit suicide. Clarke's financial woes did cause creditors to repossess his bear, forcing the cancelation of a fight.

The loss of the bear inspired Clarke to turn to wrestling bulls. Humans have been wrestling bulls for entertainment for at least 2,500 years, with ancient Thessalians performing the performing a routine in which they grabbed bulls by their horns and wrenched them to the ground. The Romans also wrestled bulls in their arenas. Julius Caesar and Augustus found the practice particularly fascinating. Augustus even had an arena specially constructed for the sport. Following Rome's collapse, humans stopped wrestling bulls directly and either killed them with weapons in bullfighting or unleashed dogs on them in bullbaiting.

Clarke revived the ancient practice for the first time in 1897, advertising that he could drag a bull down by its horns and outpull multiple horses. It is unclear what inspired him to put on the matchup. Mexican men sometimes challenged each other to grab bulls by the horns as tests of manhood, and Clarke may have witnessed one such demonstration. More likely, the American was inspired by the release of the novel *Quo Vadis* in 1896, in which the character Ursus, the son of Hercules, wrestles a bull to the ground. The fact that Clarke called himself the "Colored Hercules" speaks to this origin. Clarke may also have learned the routine from frequent opponent Romulus, who started wrestling bulls at about the same time.

Whatever the inspiration, the first performance turned out to be a disaster. Instead of dragging the bull down, Clarke ran away from his bovine opponent and only managed to grab its tail, which he held on to for dear life as the bull pulled him around the arena. The scene was so comical that locals made statues of the incident. Newspapers reported that when someone asked why he ran away, the wry Clarke replied that it was because "I can't fly."[43]

Although humiliating, Clarke's attempt to wrestle a bull could be considered the first modern public display of bulldogging. Bulldogging is a popular rodeo sport in which a human grabs a male cow by its horns and twists the animal's head to throw it off balance, forcing it to the ground. The practice resembles bulldogs taking down bulls in bullbaiting matches, hence the name. Historians generally credit Black Texan Bill Pickett as the first modern bulldogger, with his biographer, Bailey C. Hanes, proposing that Pickett wrestled a steer at a fair in 1888. Unfortunately, Hanes does not cite where he came up with this date, but the text suggests that his source was an adult recalling the fair from childhood. The next instance of Pickett wrestling a bull, and the first that can be documented, was in 1900, when Pickett took on a steer in Mexico City as part of a circus.

It is possible that Pickett came up with the idea of wrestling bulls for entertainment on his own and that he performed the feat in 1888 or another time before 1897, as Hanes argues. However, considering the date and location of his first documented show, it seems just as likely that he learned about Clarke's routine and decided to emulate it. One can imagine an undiscerning audience in Mexico City associating the two Black Americans and encouraging Pickett to do as Clarke had done. Pickett may also have learned the routine from Romulus, whom history might eventually credit for modern bulldogging. In February 1898, the Italian strongman unsuccessfully fought a bull in Juárez, with the bull tossing his opponent into the air. Although the fight took place months after Clarke's first show, Romulus claimed that he had "performed this feat repeatedly in private and three times in public in the interior of Mexico."[44]

Of course, it is possible that Clarke, Pickett and Romulus all came up with the idea to wrestle bulls on their own and that they all deserve credit for reviving the ancient sport. It might also be unfair to compare what Pickett did to what Clarke did considering that the way in which they wrestled their animals was very different. Indeed, Clarke's version of bulldogging was more dangerous than Pickett's. Pickett and modern bulldoggers start on a horse, which allows them to build momentum when they tackle their opponent, and they face off against castrated and therefore less aggressive steers. Clarke and Romulus took on bulls on foot. Whether or not Clarke deserves credit as the originator of modern bulldogging, like with *lucha libre* and Mexican boxing, he was once again at the forefront of a popular sport trend.

Clarke's first attempt to wrestle a bull was nothing to be proud of, and he obviously hoped that future fights would be less humiliating. In 1900, he and J.H. Tate, who had taken to managing the fighter, began advertising a series of fights that would take place first in Aguascalientes, then Juárez and finally El Paso. Advertisements claimed that Clarke was stronger than six horses and could catch a bull by the horns, after which Clarke "would grapple the beast and throw him."[45] El Paso newspapers published huge advertisements featuring a woodcut of an overly muscled Billy grabbing a bull by the horns and the neck, with headlines calling him the "Colored Hercules" and the "Chief of Gladiators." Promoters plastered "gorgeous life-sized lithographs" of Clarke throughout Aguascalientes, El Paso and Juárez.[46]

The day before the fight in Aguascalientes, Billy arrived at the bullring "arrayed in all his glory, his frock coat nearly reaching the ground, his Hot Springs diamond, above the size of a brick bat."[47] He was anxious to talk to reporters. Using the showman style he had developed over his years touring Mexico, he claimed that he would put on the "biggest livin' show on er'th."[48] The talk worked. By fight time on Sunday, May 9, the show had sold $2,800 in tickets.

With the crowd cheering, Billy made his entrance wearing a gold and purple coat. He strode around the bullring three times, waving to the crowd and "admiring himself" as one newspaper reported derisively.[49] Apparently management grew tired of the show because without waiting for a cue from Clarke, they had an attendant unleash the bull into the ring. One newspaper reported that at the sight of the animal "Billy's courage deserted him; cold tremor ran through his bones; his knees rattled and the bull expressed a desire to get acquainted with the great gladiator."[50] Clarke called out that he was not ready to fight, with one newspaper reporting that he claimed that his feet were frozen to the ground on account of eating too much ice cream before the fight. Six picadors and some attendants then entered the ring and helped the fighter get out before the bull charged him.

Thirty minutes later, Clarke returned carrying a tarpaulin, which he planned to drape over the bull so he could grab and throw it. Before entering the arena, however, he took a seat on the ring fence and held a fifteen-minute dialogue with himself debating whether to "disappoint the audience or hurt the bull."[51] When the presiding alderman admonished him and told him to get in the ring, Clarke entered at the farthest possible point away from the bull he could find. Instead of engaging the animal, he hid behind the tarpaulin, prompting boos from the audience. Clarke responded by daring someone from the audience to put the tarpaulin over the bull so he could throw it.

Clarke's refusal to engage proved enough for the audience. They began ripping off rails and chairs to throw into the ring. When Mexican police tried to arrest one of the offenders, an American, the audience came to his defense and refused to let him be taken. Instead, the police arrested Clarke. The authorities ended up fining him 150 pesos, and the promoters 100, and gave all receipts from the event to a local art school. Clarke tried to explain his failure by claiming that before the fight he had taken a bath in the hot springs for which Aguascalientes was named, which had left him without strength. He promised to do better at his next fight in Juárez on July 1, 1900.

However, Clarke's performance in Juárez was equally disastrous and resembled his showing in Aguascalientes so much that newspapers would conflate the two instances. As he had done before his previous fights, Clarke talked himself up in the press, claiming that he was a "professor of pugilism" and the "Colored Hercules."[52] He dismissed his previous poor performance and promised not only to fight the bull but also once again "that he would grapple the beast and throw him."[53] He may also have spoken badly about his frequent rival, Romulus, who had tried to wrestle a bull in Juárez a year and a half earlier only for the bull to toss the Italian in the air multiple times and severely injure him.

True to his word, Clarke entered the ring, and this time, he actually engaged the bull. Unfortunately, the animal was too powerful for the wrestler. It forced Clarke to the ground and trampled him. Clarke "was carried out in a precarious condition."[54]

As he often did, Clarke tried to deflect blame for his failure, saying that he had not defeated the bulls out of compassion. He claimed that the Society for the Prevention of Cruelty to Animals had bestowed an honorary membership on him prior to the fights, and he had decided not to hurt the bulls because he had become an animal lover. This was not true. Not only would Clarke continue to fight bulls, but he also had used the exact same excuse after the bull defeated him in 1897. Clarke was almost certainly using the excuse as the same sort of attention-grabbing heel tactics he used when advertising his *lucha libre* fights. If this were the case, journalists did not understand the nuance and took the bait, mocking the fighter in newspapers throughout the United States and Mexico. Even the normally sympathetic editor of the *Mexican Herald* took to piling on the defeated fighter.

Athletic Park, El Paso, Sunday, July 15, 4:30 P. M.

The Colored Hercules
Mr. Billy A. Clarke
Conquer of Romulus in Mexico cl'y
Champion Prize Fighter and All-
Round Wrestler of Mexico
The Chief of Gladiators will
Wrestle body to body with a
Fierce and Powerful Bull.

He will handle
HUGE CANNON BALLS
with astonishing rapidity,
and will pull against the
Strength of Four Borses!

The Champion Mexican Rider will
Ride a Wild Bull to a standstill.

ARENA SAFELY FENCED
No possible danger of Bull getting
out of ring.

Ticket for sale at Star Stable,
Jocky Club and Kline's Curio
Store.

The manager has secured the
Park for Sunday.

General Admission, 25c.
Grand Stand, 50c.

Advertisement for Clarke's show in El Paso. It is possible that the event was the first bull wrestling exhibition in the United States. *From El Paso Daily Herald, Saturday, July 14, 1900.*

If Clarke's intention was to sell tickets to upcoming shows, it did not work, as only "a small audience"[55] showed up to witness his fight at the Athletic Park in El Paso. The event was heavily advertised, so it is unclear if the negative stories affected attendance or if audiences had already attended the fight across the Rio Grande in Juárez. The questionable legality of the event may also have put off potential attendees. Whatever the case, the fight in El Paso was one of the few times Clarke carried through with his promises. He threw "a strong and aggressive bull" and followed up the victory by pulling four horses and lifting several iron cannonballs.[56]

The poor performances in Aguascalientes and Juárez and the low attendance in El Paso seem to have left Clarke in a financial bind. In order to recoup expenses, Clarke tried to secure a fight with Billy Smith, who had defeated Clarke six years earlier in Pachuca in the only legal boxing match in Mexico. Clarke claimed to local papers that Smith had cheated in the fight, and if given a rematch, there would be a different outcome. Now on the El Paso police force and with prizefighting still illegal in Texas, Smith refused the offer.

Clarke instead boxed the "Champion of Illinois," Fred Vance, at Chopin Hall on July 20, labeling the event as an exhibition to avoid violating Texas's prizefighting law.[57] He was joined in the performance by the Spanish skirt dancer Miss Lera and hypnotist Dr. Jiménez. It seems that attendance was once again poor, as local newspapers did not see fit to report on the show the following day. This left Billy convinced that "I didn't do nothin' at all; there aint nothin' here for me: El Paso haint got use for a nigger nohow."[58] On July 25, Clarke and his manager, J.H. Tate, boarded a train out of the city.

Clarke and Tate stopped off in Fort Worth, where they put on a show at 5:00 p.m. on August 1, 1900. Before the event, they ran advertisements claiming that Clarke was "a Strong Man from Peru" who could demonstrate amazing feats of strength and "throw down a wild bull and outpull four horses."[59] The event was to take place in the Texas and Pacific Park. General admission was twenty-five cents. Advertisements ended with "P.S.— Cowboys bring your ropes and horses and take a pull at the strong man."[60] A "considerable number" of people showed up for the event.[61]

Things started out poorly. Word had gotten around that instead of the more exotic Peru, Clarke "was just from Mexico,"[62] and "instead of a wild bull, the animal brought into the arena for Clarke to wrestle with was a small, poor steer that could hardly stand through sheer weakness."[63] The horses were equally as weak or Clarke's performance so poor that it did nothing to stymie the crowd's disappointment. Things grew worse during the weightlifting portion of the show. It had been announced that Clarke would be performing feats of strength using dumbbells weighing thirty-five pounds apiece, apparently a massive weight by the fitness standards of 1900. Clarke started his routine and acted as if he was struggling to lift the weights. The audience felt he was overacting, suspected that the weights were hollow

Mr. Billy Clarke the Strong Man from Peru

will give an exhibition of strength at the Fort Worth T. & P. park, Wednesday, August 1, at 5 p. m. Mr. Clarke will throw a large and ferocious bull which has been selected by Mr. Bud Daggett from his own herd for this occasion. He will also match his strength and pull against 4 horses free from all braces with a fair and square pull and also perform with heavy cannon Jalls.

P. S.—Cowboys bring your ropes and horses and take a pull at the strong man. General admission 25 cents, reserved seats 10 cents.

J. H. TAIT,
Manager.

Advertisement for Clarke's performance in Fort Worth. Clarke claimed to be from Peru to make his act more acceptable to white audiences. *From the* Fort Worth Morning Register, *July 29, 1900.*

and began booing. They really turned on the performer when a twelve-year-old boy walked into the arena, grabbed hold of the weights and "handled them easily in full view of the crowd."[64]

The local newspaper reported that it was at this point that the audience "rose as one body and threw themselves at the negro and his white manager."[65] The mob surrounded Clarke and Tate and began pelting them with stones. Tate managed to escape and took shelter in the small ticket office, but it seems that Clarke was unable to get away; some in the crowd began talking about lynching him. Fortunately for the showman, five policemen showed up at the scene and tried to protect him from the mob. Unfortunately, this did little to satiate the audience's bloodlust, and they began hurling stones at the policemen, with one officer receiving a shoulder injury and another a hematoma under his eye. Despite their injuries, the police managed to extract Clarke and Tate from the scene and get them in the patrol wagon to take them to jail to protect them from the mob.

Instead of giving up, the audience ran after the patrol wagon and continued to throw rocks and levy insults. Instead of dispersing when they reached the jail in the city hall, the mob grew, with a "large crowd" assembling outside the jail by evening. People tried to scramble up to the window to see the two prisoners. Many waited until the following day in the hopes that the police would release the men. Two boys showed up with "a case of eggs of doubtful age and condition" to throw.[66] Others had more violent intentions in mind. After two days, the crowd finally dispersed, and the police released Clarke and his manager. The duo "manifested a willingness to leave the city as early as possible."[67]

Billy followed up the disaster in Fort Worth with a series of short stopovers in midwestern and southern cities. He took part in a boxing match in Kansas City, which he won, and he defeated a challenger in New Orleans shortly thereafter. His stint in the South ended soon after, following stopovers in Pulaski and Hot Springs, Arkansas, where he planned to put on bulldogging exhibitions. After an initial performance, police arrested Clarke for disturbing the peace and levied a ten-dollar fine. He was released shortly thereafter and put on another show, sparsely attended, and then he received an additional fine of five dollars on September 17 for failing to receive a proper license for his performance.

The lack of revenue and fines meant that Clarke could not pay a thirty-dollar board bill to Mose Broglin, with whom he was staying, leading Broglin to confiscate his paraphernalia until he received payment. Clarke then asked a man named Ed Moore for a loan for eighty dollars to repay his debt to

Broglin. When Moore did not immediately accede to the request, Clarke forged his name on a telegram to Broglin telling him that the money was on the way and requesting that the landlord send Clarke his things. Broglin did so, but he soon discovered the deception and had Clarke arrested. Police told Clarke that he would be "released from jail on condition that he leave Pulaski and never return."[68]

Whereas Clarke's showmanship had been well received or at least tolerated in Mexico, the crowd in Fort Worth and the police in Pulaski made it very apparent that such braggadocio from an African American man was not welcome in the racist South. This was a lesson countless other people of color had learned since the end of Reconstruction, and like many others, Clarke determined that there was no place for him in the South. As such, he became among the first of some 6 million African Americans who would make the Great Migration to cities in the North, where there were better opportunities for people of color. Clarke chose to live in Chicago.

Although he would not face lynching, things were not great in his new home. Clarke disliked the cold weather, and locals discriminated against him for his time in Mexico and his wife's ancestry, with some calling him a "Mexican niggah."[69] He also had a hard time securing high-level fights, one of the reasons he had gone to Mexico in the first place. He took some matches with local African American boxers, managing to hit one opponent so hard that he knocked him over the ropes. This success led him to challenge Black Heavyweight Champion Frank "the Crafty Texan" Childs to a match in late November 1900. Childs fought "Mexican" Pete Everett, an American of Mexican descent, the following month, but he does not seem to have entertained fighting Clarke.

Clarke also had trouble finding wrestling opponents. In April 1901, his new manager, Tom Diggens, called out the white local wrestling champion John Rooney, betting $1,000 that his fighter could throw the champion. Rooney, like many white athletes at the time, "drew the color line" and refused to fight African American athletes. Rooney's manager, on the other hand, lived under the axiom that "all men are created equal on the turf or under it" and accepted the bout as long as the fight took place under traditional Greco-Roman rules.[70] Either Clarke and his team did not accept these conditions or Rooney did not like his manager speaking for him because the bout does not seem to have taken place.

On February 1, 1902, Clarke took on William Mayo of Australia in a boxing match. Mayo had just lost to Bob Fitzsimmons, one of the greatest fighters of all time. His bout with Clarke ended in a draw. In March, Clarke was once again supposed to take on Frank Childs. It appears that Klondike Haynes ruined that opportunity. Haynes was a heavyweight who beat Jack Johnson in 1899 and fought him to a draw in 1900. He lost to Johnson at the end of that year but then took a year off before defeating Clarke by points in December 1901. Their rematch was set for February 16, 1902. Clarke lost again, effectively ending any chance of taking on Childs and securing himself a place among the elite class of boxers.

It is at this point that Clarke largely disappears from recorded history. Clarke may have changed his name, as boxers sometimes did when they racked up too many losses but wanted to continue to compete. A career in boxing may also have begun to take its toll, leaving Clarke with brain damage and unable to compete. It is also possible that Clarke gave in to drinking, gambling or the personal demons that had begun to haunt him in Mexico.

Whatever the case, Clarke's legacy would live on in Mexico, at least for a time. In certain areas of the country, residents used the phrase "stronger than Billy Clark" as a sign of physical admiration for years after Clarke left.[71] Human-on-animal wrestling continued to grow in popularity, a reality seen on the Texas-Mexico border. In Juárez on March 11, 1902, Clarke's rival, Romulus, now calling himself the "Mexican Sandow," "wrestled with an infuriated bull and held him by the horns until the beast was conquered."[72] Bill Pickett took on an elk at the El Paso fair in 1906. Although the animal had "large sharp antlers that could rip a man in half," Pickett managed to subdue the beast after a ten-minute battle.[73] Of course, Pickett would become most famous as a bulldogger who wrestled bulls and steers, a routine he may have adapted from one of Clarke's performances.

Clarke certainly played a part in making boxing and wrestling the popular sports they are today in Mexico, although his influence is immeasurable. There is no way to know how many future *lucha libre* performers witnessed Clarke's braggadocio as children and imitated it when they became fighters in adulthood, but there were almost certainly some. Clarke's boxing clubs also likely turned out fighters who then opened their own clubs to train fighters, laying the foundations for the eventual acceptance of boxing in Mexico. Famed Mexican boxer Policarpo Santa Maria would later credit Clarke's visits to his mother's lunch counter and discussions of boxing as an impetus for beginning his own boxing career.

Clarke may also have encouraged other African American athletes to move to Mexico to ply their craft. In 1913, heavyweight boxing champion Jack Johnson moved to Mexico to escape a conviction of violating the Mann Act, which historians generally interpret as an unjustified charge levied against Johnson because white boxers could not beat him. While in Mexico, Johnson befriended elites, taught boxing and put on strongman and bullfighting exhibitions. He also boxed, taking five matches from 1919 to 1920. By that time, Mexico had lifted its ban on prizefighting. Johnson's biographers credit their subject with opening the nation to boxing and athletes of African ancestry. In reality, Billy Clarke preceded him by twenty years.

CHAPTER 4

IN THE LION'S DEN

In March 1902, Jim Jeffries and Bob Fitzsimmons tried to test Mexico's ban on boxing and hold a fight in the Juárez bullring. It did not happen. Mexican legal authorities refused to entertain the matchup. The month after the Jeffries and Fitzsimmons fight fell through, the same venue would host a different style of fight—another battle between an African lion and a Mexican bull. In some ways, the bout was not special. There had been prior lion-bull battles in Mexico, and the circumstances that led to the fight were not particularly unique. However, the public reaction to the fight, and the way in which the press reported on it, varied greatly from the bouts between the lion Parnell, the bear Ramadan and the bull Panthera just seven years before, providing insight into dramatic changes in media and public sentiment at the start of the twentieth century.

The 1902 lion-bull fight was not the only one to take place in Mexico following the Parnell-Panthera battle. In 1890, American colonel Robert C. Pate moved to Mexico hoping to make money. Prior to this time, he had amassed a small fortune running a horse track and keno parlor in St. Louis, but recent elections had put anti-gambling government officials in power who threatened to shut his businesses down. Pate left with his money, opened a nail factory in Monterrey, Mexico, and sold out after a few years for a substantial profit. Instead of returning to the United States, Pate moved to Mexico City, where he opened a racetrack near the Indianilla streetcar station and ran daily horse races.

Initially the track did well, bringing in substantial gambling revenue, but in 1898, Pate was hit by accusations of race fixing, eroding confidence among gamblers and forcing Pate to suspend horse racing for the near future. Pate tried to replace the horse races with traditional American sports. He held a football match between the University of Texas and the University of Missouri, but Mexican audiences did not come. Like boxing, they found football to be brutal and boring.

Pate found an alternative form of entertainment when the African American entertainer Billy Clarke performed at his racetrack in 1898. It is unclear how the two met, but the colonel may have attended one of Clarke's underground boxing matches or one of his variety shows at the boxer's Olympic Club in Mexico City and noticed the performer's appeal with audiences. Whatever the case, the colonel commissioned Clarke for at least two shows at Indianilla. In one, Clarke fought a bear, and in another he took on a bull. Even though Clarke ran away from the bull he was supposed to fight in the latter performance, both events seem to have sold well.

Either inspired by Clarke's performance or seeing how the nearby Gran Circo Teatro drew crowds, Pate determined to re-create Rome in Mexico City by staging four fights to the death between lions and bulls. The promoter suspected that Mexicans would attend because it resembled their traditional bullfights and the bear and bull fights that used to take place in California. The bizarre appealed to Americans in Mexico, and because many were fascinated with Mexican culture, a sales pitch that the event was uniquely Hispanic would draw those seeking to learn more about their adopted country of residence.

Aware of laws against prizefighting, Pate sought permission from local politicians to hold his fights. Because there was a push to promote tourism in Mexico City through pageantry, he received approval in late March 1898. However, before the program could go on, Pate had to submit a performance bond with the government guaranteeing that the four promised shows would actually take place. To ensure public safety, he also had to allow government inspectors to exam his cage.

Building the cage proved expensive, as was buying the two lions and multiple bulls that would participate in the show. Perhaps because Mexico did not have vaudeville performers traveling throughout the country like the United States, Pate had to purchase two lions from overseas at great cost. However, Pate hoped to recoup expenses by charging an expensive five dollars for general admission and ten for reserved seating. To draw buyers, Pate advertised a "unique battle royal!"[74] The marketing worked, as the event sold out, with tickets selling to both Mexican elites and American expatriates.

Reflecting trends that would later be seen in the United States, newspapers in Mexico had mixed emotions about the prospective battles. One writer for the *Mexican Herald* deemed the event a "barbarous revival of the Roman Circus."[75] Still another—with Spain and the United States preparing to go to war—suggested that it would be more humane to have the Spanish colony in Mexico City fight the American colony. Another defended the upcoming fight on practical terms—it was the same as feeding the lion in the wild.

When the fights finally took place in early April 1898, they proved anticlimactic. The bull smashed the first lion against the side of the cage as soon as it entered, after which the lion crumpled to the ground and refused to fight any longer. The bull also seemed equally disinterested in furthering the contest. In promising four fights, Pate had expected each lion to win at least one matchup, but with the first lion already severely injured, he was forced to put in the second lion and hope that it could take down three bulls in succession. It could not. Once again, the bull drove his opponent into the cage, leading the second lion to give up and the second bull to stop fighting. Reflecting what happened to Parnell, Pate had his attendants poke the bull with a pike and wave a flag behind the lion. Finally, the bull charged, goring, stomping and killing the lion. Onlookers would later lasso and drag its body around the bullring.

Newspaper reaction to the event varied, but most mocked what took place in one form or another. Some debated the perceived value of the fights. The *Mexican Herald* felt that the event was "an exciting and interesting afternoon's amusement" and worth the price of admission.[76] *El Imparcial* was less impressed, complaining that two of the promised four fights did not take place and that the lions did not put up much of a fight in the two that did. A writer for *El Nacional* spoke to morality in calling the event "barbarous, more cruel and decadent than Rome" and blamed Americans for bringing such spectacles to Mexico.[77] Unlike the bullfights usually seen in their country, Pate's event lacked honor, structure and tradition. Even *El Nacional* could not resist entering the debate over value, calling the whole fiasco a hoax. Perhaps most bizarrely, a furniture seller took advantage of the controversy by releasing an advertisement that declared "a war against furniture" and stated, "The lions would not fight the bull yesterday...but I will defy all prices in furniture."[78]

Because there had been only two fights instead of the promised four, Pate lost his performance bond. Although what exactly this meant is unclear, he likely had to forfeit much or all the gate. The promoter cursed his luck and blamed the lions' poor performance on still being uneasy from their sea voyage to Mexico. Pate learned a lesson from the event. Lions and bulls were too unpredictable. He turned to full-time greyhound racing in which the speedy dog breed chased down six-pound rabbits. Unfortunately for Pate, his reputation for fixing horse races carried over to his new endeavor, and thanks to a variety of other factors, the Indianilla racetrack failed to make money. He left Mexico in 1900 and went on to start a roulette parlor in St. Louis.

Either speaking to turn-of-the-century media circulation or the fact that the United States was on the verge of war with Spain, American newspapers did not report on Pate's failure. Nor would they give much attention to a lion-bull fight put on by Daniel Boone, now calling himself a professor, in Juárez in 1898. The fight involved a lion named Nero, not to be confused with the lion Nero that Bob Fitzsimmons brought to Juárez as a pet in 1896 only to see the lion escape and terrorize the town before the boxer could recapture it. Nor should Boone's Nero be confused with the lion Nero that bit off his trainer's head during a head-in-the-mouth trick gone wrong in Virginia in 1898 or the lion Nero that would later escape from a Juárez bullring and cause a massive panic. Instead, Boone's Nero, unlike Parnell before him, refused to fight when faced against a bull, prompting the governor of Chihuahua to call off the fight.

If newspapers had covered Pate and Boone's lion-bull fight failures, it might have prevented Arthur J. Morrison from attempting to put on a similar event on the Texas-Mexico border just four years later. Morrison was an Arkansas native who moved in 1880 to South Africa, where he spent nineteen years mining in the Kimberley diamond mines and trading from Cape Town to Sansidar. Whether through trade or trapping, around 1898, Morrison came into possession of two African lion cubs, one female and one male. He named the male King Lobengula, after a Ndebele king who allowed outsiders to mine and trade on his people's land. The two animals grew quickly, with the male developing an intensely black mane. One report said that by adulthood Lobengula weighed 675 pounds, which if true would make him one of the heaviest lions on record. In 1899, Morrison; his wife, Sybil; and the two lions left Africa for Los Angeles, stopping at Australia, New Zealand and Hawaii along the way.

Once in Southern California, the couple opened the Lion's Den café near Westlake Park (now MacArthur Park), where they sold soda water and ice cream. The lions sat in a cage in the yard of the venue as a draw for customers. On weekends, the Morrisons also opened part of their establishment to dancing and, as their neighbors suspected, illegal alcohol sales and prostitution. Many dance halls of the time allowed enterprising women free entry on the condition that the women sought out dance partners among the male guests. In order to gain the privilege of dancing, the man had to pay for a drink for the woman. The owners of the dance hall would mark down how many drinks the woman received and pay her a portion of the sales at the end of the night. The women sometimes made additional money by bringing intoxicated johns back to their homes where they charged for sex.

Within a few weeks of opening, neighbors began to complain about the suspected prostitution and the drunken men who stumbled out of the dance hall and passed out on their lawns. However, the neighbors' biggest issue was the lions. The smell of the lions could be overwhelming, and their "continual roaring" often carried on well into the night.[79] Local residents also felt that the lions' cage was insecure and that it was only a matter of time before the animals escaped and hurt someone.

The police responded to the complaints by issuing Morrison an arrest warrant for "maintaining a nuisance in the park."[80] Morrison fought the charge by claiming that his wife was the owner of the animals in the hopes that the neighbors and police would be hesitant to prosecute a woman. The tactic apparently worked for this particular offense, but the police found other reasons to fine the couple. They brought them up on charges of disturbing the peace, running a dance hall without paying the proper tax and selling liquor without a license.

The Morrisons beat the dance hall charge by requesting a jury trial in which they claimed that they were not holding public dances but rather private programs meant to teach the art of dancing. They responded to the alcohol charge by selling Los Angeles Brewing Company "temperance brew" beer, purported to be non-intoxicating.[81] After police officers sampled the beverages and found themselves inebriated, they arrested the couple and charged them a $100 fine. This led the Morrisons to sue the Los Angeles Brewing Company for $5,000, with Mrs. Morrison claiming that her arrest had caused "grievous humiliation and indignity and mental injury." Her "sensitive nature" meant that she also experienced "physical and mental suffering" due to her arrest.[82]

Newspapers are silent on whether the Morrisons won their civil suit, but the fact that in 1902 Mr. Morrison found himself betting exactly $5,000 on one of his lions to beat a bull in a cage fight indicates that they did.

The circumstances that led to the event are unclear, but Morrison would later claim that it had been his neighbors' complaints about the lions' roars and the apparently unavoidable disturbing the peace charges that came with them that prompted the fight. The death of the female lion in November 1901 also likely played a part in the decision. Apparently, the novelty of the lions had already been wearing off before the lioness's death, and Morrison felt that a single lion would be less of a draw than two, so he decided to sell King Lobengula. After finding no buyers, Morrison concocted the idea of taking the lion to Juárez.

To facilitate the fight, Morrison contacted Dr. Mariano Samaniego, a local politician and pharmacist in Juárez who owned bullfighting privileges in the city. Samaniego approved of Morrison's plan, but owing to a recent incident in the bullring, the governor of Chihuahua had suspended his license—he would need special permission to put on the fight. On March 31, 1902, Americans in attendance at a Juárez bullfight cheered when a bull tossed a matador into the air, lacerated his right leg and hip and stripped him of his clothes. Seeing this as disrespect for their sport, Mexican attendees took offense; according to one report, "It looked as though there would be a collision between the two races."[83]

Although a riot was averted, the governor believed that the incident and the poor bullfighting that was regularly taking place in Juárez had caused the national sport to "fall into disrepute." He also decried the stunts put on by Juárez promoters to "lure Americans to the games across the river," citing an incident from two years before wherein promoters had put on "an exhibition of a negro wrestling with a bull."[84] Somehow Samaniego was able to assure the governor and the mayor of Juárez that a fight between a lion and bull was not a stunt, and the two gave their permission for the event to proceed. The mayor even promised to attend.

Samaniego and Morrison scheduled the fight to take place on April 13, 1902. While Morrison secured a means to transport King Lobengula from California to Juárez, Samaniego set about finding a bull, taking "the greatest care to get the most ferocious one possible."[85] After locating a candidate, and perhaps having learned from previous lion-bull fights, promoters shaved the tips of the bull's horns to prevent it from making quick work of the lion. Samaniego also oversaw construction of a twenty-five-by-thirty-foot circular cage at a cost of $1,500.

Whereas Parnell's 1895 fight with Panthera relied primarily on word of mouth to sell tickets and only a few periodicals sent reporters, the 1902 battle received much more press attention. Journalism in the United States had seen a period of rapid evolution in the late nineteenth century after certain entrepreneurial newspaper owners realized that they would make more money with headlines promising violence and the bizarre. Newspapers became more sensationalistic, printing more articles concerning the margins of society and telling stories that held little importance to daily life but appealed to prurient instincts. When real-life events proved to be mundane, some newspapers, particularly those in eastern cities, often sacrificed the truth for the dramatic.

Newspapers and magazines in 1902 also featured more photographs and detailed drawings than they had just seven years before. Before the turn of the twentieth century, only the biggest newspapers in the United States had the ability to print photographs; these photographs were often of low quality, and long exposure times meant that action shots were blurry. Things began to change in 1897, when the *New York Tribune* became the first newspaper in the United States to adapt halftone to the rotary press. Halftone images were of higher quality and allowed for clearer renderings of objects in motion, meaning that the *Tribune* could depict real life much better than its competitors. Other major newspapers followed suit, and by 1902, most major publications in the United States featured photographs in their pages.

This media evolution meant that while newspapers carried no photographs of the Parnell, Ramadan and Panthera bouts, from the beginning, King Lobengula's fight with the bull received extensive visual documentation. One journalist went so far as to report that "the revival of the sport of gladiator days of Rome is being widely discussed and papers all over the country are sending in advance orders to have the fight fully covered and pictures taken."[86] Multiple photographers showed up to document the event. One photographer, Feldman, arranged to have his camera placed on the cage to "get perfect photographs of the fight as it progresses."[87] Morrison stood in the lion's cage and posed so artists could draw him.

Morrison and the Juárez promoters supplemented the attention by advertising heavily in border newspapers and passing out pamphlets in El Paso that leaned into the comparisons to Roman times. According to advertisements, tickets buyers would enjoy the sport of Roman Caesars. Promoters promised "One Brief Hour in a Roman Amphitheatre," "a grand spectacle" and "A Roman Holiday." In a questionable bit of marketing considering that most in the United States and Mexico were Christian, one pamphlet noted that "our lion will rave here as his ancestors did in the Colosseum when either the holy Christian Martyr, or the bull or the tiger were made to cope with his fury."[88] Perhaps to offset the disturbing mental

Left: Newspapers carried full-page editorials describing the various lion-bull fights that took place in Mexico, often including vivid drawings and photographs of the events. *From the* Cleveland Leader, *May 11, 1902.*

Opposite: Newspapers frequently compared the animal combat events of the border to ancient Roman spectacles. *From the* Cincinnati Enquirer, *April 14, 1902.*

imagery this description invoked, the pamphlet promised that spectators would be safe.

Gambling parlors in the United States and Mexico even took bets on the event. Regular attendees to the bullfights believed that the bull would win, having frequently witnessed bulls taking down horses much bigger than a lion. American gamblers who had never seen a bullfight and who were apparently unaware of previous matchups between bulls and lions heavily favored Lobengula, resulting in 65-20 odds in favor of the lion. Morrison had regularly seen lions take down African oxen twice their size, so he too favored Lobengula, placing $5,000 on his animal to emerge victorious.

When fight day arrived on April 13, attendees came from all over. Newspapers reported that "the greater part of the audience in the great amphitheater surrounding the ring was from New Mexico, west Texas, Chihuahua and vicinity. Gray-haired Mexicans walked four days from the interior of Chihuahua to witness the exhibition."[89] However, another said that it was "primarily an American audience" and that a quarter of the

A BATTLE FIT FOR A NERO.

A View of the Bull—The Survivor of Several Fights—As He Appeared in a Former Contest

crowd was American women.[90] As had happened in the matchup between Panthera and Parnell, attendants first brought the bull to the cage and then wheeled in a smaller cage bearing King Lobengula. Unlike Panthera, who was eager to fight and bent the bars to his cage trying to get to his opponent, the bull in the 1902 contest did not appear agitated or prepared for combat.

What happened when attendees opened the gates separating the two animals is difficult to discern using newspaper accounts, and the discrepancy in reporting provides insight into the state of media in the early twentieth century. Some Texas newspapers, including the *Daily Advocate* of Victoria, Texas, portrayed the fight as having little action. King Lobengula refused to fight, and so did the bull. They were both so non-threatening that an ornery mule could defeat them both. The *El Paso Daily Times* said that the fight was "exceedingly tame, as the lion refused to fight and the bull's horns were sawed off."[91] The *Galveston Tribune* agreed, saying that the action was "sanguinary."[92] Although it is difficult to assign motive, local papers might have been trying to downplay events because newspapers outside of the state had taken to portraying Texas and specifically El Paso as violent and backward. Defending itself, the *El Paso Daily Times* said, "Why should El Paso be called bloodthirsty because Juárez indulges in brutal sports."[93]

The story of the fight was very different in eastern newspapers. According to a report that multiple newspapers carried, when attendants opened his cage, Lobengula took the initiative, leaping on the bull's back and "landing like a thunderbolt."[94] His claws tore into the bovine's sides, and his fangs closed in on its opponent's throat. The bull managed to shake the lion off and then throw him "backward and upward repeatedly" with its horns.[95] Twice more the lion managed to escape this treatment and take the bull's back, but each time the bull shook him off and gored him.

The sensationalist *Cleveland Leader* was among those that featured a dramatic version of the fight. It carried a nearly full-page step-by-step breakdown, supplemented with three photographs, profiles of each of the fighters and a drawing of the animals tussling. According to the newspaper, the fighting was "exciting" and "thick and fast."[96] While the bull appeared to be doing the most damage to those away from the cage, up close, the lion was doing work on his opponent's interior with his jaws and claws. This more titillating version of events led one Texas newspaper to note that "the Juarez fights are not bloody until they get on the wires going to eastern papers."[97]

Many newspapers carried a version of events put out by the *San Francisco Examiner*. Although not from the East, the William Randolph Hearst–owned paper was equally sensational, but it also used its stories to opine on morality. Accordingly, the *Examiner* emphasized the cruelty of the lion-bull fight and blamed the Americans in attendance for it happening in the first place. According to the *Examiner*, there was a pause in the action when both exhausted animals refused to fight. At this point, a Mexican policeman opened the lion's cage in the hopes that the animal would return to it and the match would be called off. Morrison shooed him away and approached the side of the cage, prompting to lion to run to him. Having been raised by him since it was a cub, the lion expected protection. Instead, "his master cruelly beat him with a long club and goaded him with iron rods." Indeed, throughout the fight, Morrison also "threw acid on the lion to enrage him."[98]

The *Examiner* and most newspapers that carried the fight admitted that the lion ultimately lost. As one reporter described the scene, "He was gored time and time again by his fierce antagonist and tossed about on the enraged bull's horns like a stuffed animal."[99] Eventually, the bull caved in the lion's ribs and, judging by the blood coming from the lion's mouth, punctured a

„Lion & Bull" fight, Ciudad Juarez, Mexico, 1902.

In the late nineteenth and early twentieth centuries, photographic postcards often featured violent and fantastic images. This one depicts King Lobengula facing off against a bull in Juárez. *Texas States Archives.*

lung. The lion, however, continued to put up a fight for forty minutes until the bull stepped on his leg and broke it, preventing the lion from evading his opponent. As in the fight between Parnell and Panthera, the bull's attacks did more damage, and eventually "the lion was completely vanquished in spirit and physical strength and injured fatally."[100] This was untrue, as King Lobengula survived, but he was in such poor condition that either the mayor or the local police called off the fight.

The disparity in reporting continued well after the fight. Likely owing to the increased influence of the Humane Society and the Society for the Prevention of Cruelty to Animals, many newspapers vilified Morrison and the promoters. The *Newton Daily Herald* of Kansas called it "A Sickening Spectacle Worthy of Decadent Rome."[101] Another said that it was "the cruelest and most revolting exhibition ever witnessed on the border by an American audience."[102] The *Los Angeles Herald* remarked, "It is humiliating to have the news go abroad to the world that a Los Angeles man was responsible for the sickening exhibition that that occurred last Sunday."[103]

Newspapers blamed the Americans in the audience, with the *San Francisco Examiner* printing a byline that claimed, "Americans Applaud Brutal Show: It Disgusts Mexicans."[104] The women who attended faced particularly virulent backlash from the press. A writer to the *El Paso Herald* said that female attendees "left their womanhood and modesty" and "debased" their children.[105] One columnist for the *Beaumont Enterprise* noted, "A woman who could enjoy a scrap between animals would likely make a rip-roaring wife slamming doors like a hurricane and screeching like a parrot; the other kind, those that can speak soft and low like the murmuring of zephyrs and can close a door without waking up the dead do not go to bullfights, but stay at home crooning cradle songs and frying meat."[106]

Multiple newspapers even went so far as to predict that the fight signaled the downfall of civilization. The *Brownsville Herald* reported that the crowd had "watched the scene with all the zeal of a barbarian and cheered the bloody combatants with all the wild enthusiasm and gusto of the most blood-thirsty Roman." The *Herald* lamented that "our modern humane education" is giving way to a "reveling in gore, and this total lack of humane sensibilities."[107] The *Wichita Beacon* compared the event to what happened in the days of Nero and said that people's reaction to animal fighting was that same as it was to lynching: they denounced the practice when it happened somewhere else but joined in when given the chance. The *El Paso Times* concluded that "revivals of the customs of Nero's time appear to be fashionable. Juarez started off with a bull and lion fight and North Carolina follows by making a suicide a social function."[108] Indeed, that same month, a wealthy farmer from North Carolina named Allen Cogswell informed his friends that he planned to publicly kill himself and invited those he knew to attend. The *Times* compared the event to Pretonius, the Roman patrician who killed himself in front of dinner guests.

Owing to the backlash, one newspaper predicted that "no other [animal fight] will probably be given at Juarez."[109] This proved not to be the case. The week of June 15, 1902, promoters advertised that there would be a "thrilling fight" between a badger and a bulldog followed by dancing in the bullring dancing pavilion.[110] Reserved seats went for twenty-five cents, while general admission was ten cents.

Morrison also did not seem to have been affected by the bad press, as he was already making plans to fight Lobengula once the lion recovered from its wounds. According to Morrison, his lion had lost because the species only ever fought at night, so if the fight time changed, so would the result. To make the animal more vicious in the cage, Morrison gave Lobengula nothing but water for several days and then threw a small calf or a goat into the cage to get the lion used to tearing apart four legged animals. The *El Paso Times* mockingly pointed out that this tactic had been tried with Parnell years before, but Parnell, which the paper felt was a much better competitor, still lost its bout with Panthera.

There is no indication that the water deprivation technique worked and little evidence that Lobengula ever fought again, although Morrison claimed that he did. Indeed, upon returning to Los Angeles in December 1902, Morrison swore that King Lobengula's first fight with a bull had been an aberration, and he had since taken the animal to other parts of Mexico, where the lion had successfully defeated seventeen wild bulls. There are many reasons to doubt Morrison's claim. First, there are no newspaper reports in Mexico or the United States describing these fights. Second, considering the previous record between lions and bulls and the poor state the Lobengula was in after his first bout, it is unlikely that the lion could survive a single additional bout, nonetheless wrack up seventeen wins. Third, Morrison was not the most honest person.

The promoter's dishonesty is evidenced by another tale and animal Morrison brought back from Mexico. When returning to Los Angeles, Morrison brought a seventy-three-pound, twenty-two-inch-tall horse he named Lilliputian with him. He claimed that he had acquired the animal while in Tampico and that it had been the property of a Mexican man who visited an island "off the South American coast between Guatemala and Samoa" where "the natives there worship these animals."[111] The man stole two of the miniature horses in an elaborate heist and escaped back to Mexico, where he sold one to Morrison, who began to call the animal Lilliputian. After one newspaper wryly noted of the thief, "as he immediately disappeared there seems to be no reason for doubting the assertion,"[112] Morrison added the detail that the thief had been fatally shot while escaping the island, and that was why he could not be found.

Morrison exhibited the new horse and his lion at various venues throughout California. In August 1903, after bringing the lion to a fair near Santa Rosa, Morrison arranged to have a deliveryman drop the animal off at the Southern Pacific Railroad to be shipped to Santa Cruz, where Morrison would be waiting. The railroad refused to ship the dangerous animal and stowed it instead in a warehouse, where it roared all night. Having already left the city, Morrison did not immediately pick the animal up, and the railroad did not know what to do with it, so it allowed a local piano dealer to display the animal in his store window. Morrison waited for days worrying about his animal—although apparently not worried enough to contact the shipping company—only to read what happened in a San Francisco newspaper. When Morrison finally showed up, the piano dealer refused to release Lobengula until Morrison paid the $26.75 he had spent for the lion's upkeep.

Morrison either paid the bill or his threats to sue over the matter convinced the store owner to release the animal into his custody, as Morrison was able to take possession of Lobengula. However, in 1905, he decided to sell the lion to the City of Los Angeles for $1,000. The city put the lion in a local park, where it became a popular attraction, although he frequently tried to kill the zookeepers who attended to him. At one point, he bit into a keeper's arm. Little information is available on Morrison, but he still lived with Sybil in Los Angeles in 1910. Apparently, one of the couple's schemes had worked in their favor because neither had a job, and they lived off Morrison's personal income.

CHAPTER 5

RIOT AND REVENGE
AT THE 1904 WORLD'S FAIR

A third performer to pass through the Juárez bullring in the first years of the twentieth century was Spanish bullfighter Manuel Cervera, and like Clarke and Morrison, he sought to gain money by fighting animals. What set Cervera apart from Morrison was that whereas the Americans tried to make money by traveling to Mexico, Cervera brought his sport, bullfighting, from Mexico to the United States.

In April 1898, the United States went to war with Spain under the mistaken belief that the Spanish had been behind the explosion of the USS *Maine* in Havana Harbor and in the hopes of assisting Cuban revolutionaries in their bid for independence. In one of the first acts of war, the United States sent a naval fleet to Cuba in the hopes of isolating the colony from the mother country. Spain sent its own fleet under Admiral Pascual Cervera to defend Cuban waters, but the Spanish navy was outgunned by the Americans; upon arriving in Cuba in May, Cervera had to pull his ships into Santiago's harbor for shelter and refueling. Because Santiago was short on coal, the operation took days, allowing the Americans to blockade the harbor and trap Cervera's fleet inside. For the next two months, the Spanish navy tried to blast its way out, but the American navy was too organized to allow for an escape. Finally, on July 3, Cervera saw what he thought was an opportunity to reach open waters and sailed his ships out of the harbor. Unfortunately for the admiral, the Americans quickly surrounded him, destroyed his fleet and took the admiral as a prisoner.

The course of the war was similar in other areas of the world, as the Americans made short work of the Spanish military in the Philippines and Puerto Rico, forcing Spain to ask for a ceasefire in August 1898. In December 1898, Spain recognized Cuban independence and surrendered Guam, Puerto Rico and the Philippines to the United States, opening additional Latin American and Asian markets to American goods. The acquisition of so much territory and the economic benefits it provided quickly changed public sentiment in the United States. Previously, Americans largely viewed imperialism and colonialism unfavorably, but many now felt that it was their nation's responsibility to bring what they believed to be their superior government, economics and culture to other shores.

At almost the same time that Admiral Cervera was doing his best to fend off the American fleet, his nephew, Manuel Cervera Prieto, was entertaining a group of American businessmen at a private party just outside Mexico City. The host was Thomas D. Martínez Cardeza, the Philadelphia-raised son of a wealthy Spanish businessman, who had come to Mexico in 1898 in search of business opportunities. (Martínez Cardeza was so wealthy that he and his mother would later occupy the second-most luxurious suite on the *Titanic*.) It was not long before Martínez Cardeza became enthralled with Mexican culture, including bullfighting, and in the hopes of introducing his fellow Americans to the sport, he used his wealth to rent out a bullring and hire Cervera and a troupe of female matadors to dispatch three bulls. As far as the Americans could tell, the matadors did their jobs well, eliminating the bulls in short order.

Most of Cervera's audiences were more discerning than the Americans he entertained that day, and many of his fellow bullfighters regarded him as a poor example of their profession. Cervera was born to a wealthy family in Barcelona. Coming from prominence afforded more opportunities than most in Spain. He could have joined the Spanish navy, as his famous paternal uncle had done, or he could become a bullfighter like Diego "Cuatro Dedos" Prieto from his mother's side of the family. Cervera chose the latter and adopted the diminutive "Cerverita" when bullfighting likely as an homage to his paternal uncle. He also earned the name "the pretty bullfighter" for his good looks.[113]

When later asked, Cervera claimed that he was a naturally talented bullfighter and that he quickly became so famous that he was "a favorite of the king of Spain," Alfonso XIII.[114] In reality, the king had never seen Cervera perform, and according to some reports, the bullfighter rarely performed publicly in Spain because he was not very good. This lack of talent forced Cervera to do what many inferior bullfighters had to do: he set off for the Americas, where Spanish colonialism had made bullfighting popular, but the population was less discerning about the particulars of the sport than they were in the mother country. The simple fact that Cervera had a Spanish pedigree afforded him greater respect than local American talent. Cervera chose to make a career in Mexico because that is where his relative Cuatro Dedos had had success, and his lineage would likely open many doors in the former Spanish colony.

Unfortunately for the would-be bullfighter, his lack of talent was evident even in Mexico. One newspaper whimsically reported of a bullfight in Bucareli, "Cerverita covered himself with ignominy. He displayed great timidity. His first bull he mangled atrociously and finally it had to be withdrawn from the ring alive." The writer noted that the two other bullfighters featured at this event were new to the sport, but in spite of this, the *novilleros* "acquitted themselves better than the admiral's namesake."[115] In another instance, Cervera got into an argument with a fellow bullfighter who was to perform a pole stunt, and both refused to give up the pole. Cervera finally won the argument but was unable to perform the stunt because the bull caught him on a horn and threw him, although he was not seriously hurt. Still another time, Cervera attacked a fellow bullfighter because he got more applause from the crowd than him.

In another unfortunate performance in October 1898, Cervera delivered a thrust that only went a short distance into a bull and did not kill it. The bull shook off the sword; it flew into the crowd and embedded itself in the upper thigh of an audience member, Manuel Zehfuss from Germany, inflicting "a deep gash in the soft part of the leg from which the hemorrhage was most copious."[116] Authorities arrested Cervera, and on October 17, he went before a judge, who ruled that the bullfighter was not at fault because the spectators knew the inherent risk in attending the fight, establishing a legal precedent. Although he escaped charges, the incident appears to have damaged his reputation. On Sunday, February 19, 1899, two bullfighters visiting from Spain refused to perform with Cervera because "they could not think of demeaning themselves by appearing in the arena on an equal footing with a mere novice such as they declared Cervera to be."[117] The bullfight was canceled.

Somehow, perhaps owing to his family's wealth or the dearth of quality bullfighters in Mexico, Cervera continued to find jobs, and around 1900, he began performing regularly in Juárez. Cervera had either improved enough with experience or the other bullfighters in the town were so bad that he soon came to be regarded as one of the better bullfighters in the border community. His success may also have owed to the multitude of Americans who crossed from El Paso to attend bullfights and who were even more uneducated about the sport than Juárez residents. They could not tell the difference between a good bullfighter and a bad one, and many did not care. Cervera's name also carried weight with the Americans considering that in the years since the Spanish-American War, many in the United States had come to regard Admiral Cervera as a Tecumseh-esque "worthy opponent" who, although an enemy, had acted with honor during the war. The Cervera name carried prestige.

Cervera capitalized on his family name and newfound success by transitioning from bullfighter to bullfighting manager, a move that was facilitated by marriage to Marian Abell, an actress from Baltimore who played the titular Carmen in a touring theater production. The origins of their relationship differ across sources, but it seems that Abell saw one of Cervera's bullfighting shows in Spain; the two met again when Cervera attended one of her plays in Arizona. Considering that *Carmen* involves a woman falling in love with a Spanish bullfighter, it may have been kismet that Abell and Cervera fell for each other. When Abell later came to El Paso, Cervera asked for her hand in marriage, and the two wed sometime around 1900.

Having grown up in the United States and possessing theater experience, Abell Cervera helped her husband hire bullfighters who specifically appealed to American audiences. This included a cadre of attractive female bullfighters, who were not good at fighting bulls, but they brought audiences because American newspapers liked writing about their "plump shoulders."[118]

One of Cervera's biggest draws was the self-proclaimed "American bullfighter" Carleton Bass.[119] Bass's title was misleading. Having been born in Ireland, Bass was not an American, and according to newspapers, "he was never thought to be a bullfighter in any sense of the term for he lacked the nerve that is needed by those that follow that hazardous calling."[120] However, this mattered little to American audiences, who wanted to see one of their own compete, and Bass proved to be a big draw in Juárez, at least initially. Even the untrained American eyes knew that he was not very good after he fell attempting to jump over one bull and missed stabbing another in the back and instead hit its thigh. The injured and angry animal chased Bass out of the arena while the audience rained boos, trash and anything else they could get their hands on down on the fleeing bullfighter. Bass refused to come back out to finish the fight.

The "American Matador"
Carleton Bass (left) and
Manuel Cervera (right).
From the Inter Ocean,
August 15, 1904.

Many of Cervera's other bullfighters experienced injuries, and still others only took on weak bulls, leading one person to comment that the performers in Juárez were talentless "cowboys or 'greasers'" who fought Texas steers, not true wild bulls.[121] The Mexican government even took notice of the poor performances and threatened to shut down the shows to preserve the honor of the national sport. Despite these criticisms, Cervera continued to profit because undiscerning Americans kept coming across the bridge. So many attended shows in early 1903 that the owner of the bullfighting rights to the city, Dr. Mariano Samaniego, began construction of a new, permanent bullring in Juárez.

Americans poured into the new structure looking more for spectacle than art. Cervera obliged. For example, after shows, he would place a portion of the gate receipts in a box, which he tied to the shaved horns of a small bull that he loosed in the arena at the end of bullfights. The audience was invited to try to grab the box.[122] Apparently the bullfighter did not count on the American desire to be part of the show because in December 1903, one audience member grabbed a banderilla and sunk it into the bull's shoulders. "With a roar and a tremendous leap," the bull "cleared the grandstand railing, landing on his haunches in the spectator's booths." The animal

The newly constructed Juárez bullring. *El Paso Public Library.*

then began to trample women and children until Cervera showed up and "plunged his sword into its vitals, and the beast rolled over and died in the grandstand." Unfortunately, an older Mexican gentleman "slipped and fell in the blood of the dead bull. He rolled over and over down the steps until he landed within a few feet of the conquered beast."[123]

In spite of this absurdity, Americans continued to show up for the fights, convincing Cervera that if he put on a performance within the United States, it would bring even more money than he could make in Juárez. Unfortunately, Cervera knew from personal experience that finding a venue that would allow bullfighting was difficult, especially for a non-native English speaker without surplus capital. In August 1902, Cervera took out a $145 loan from attorney Joseph Wheless in the hopes of using the money to put on a bullfighting exhibition in St. Louis. Cervera secured a venue and sold numerous tickets, but locals railed against the upcoming event. One even commented, "Why stop at bull-baiting? Let us have bear-baiting, rat-killing, chicken mains [*sic*], badger-drawing, and dog fighting. Think what crowds could be drawn to the Fair were such a varied programme as this offered."[124] The complaints led the city to pass an ordinance banning bullfighting, leaving Cervera unable to pay back Wheless. Wheless tried to seize Cervera's expensive costume, which the bullfighter had used as collateral, but the bullfighter hid it and escaped town before he could be arrested for secreting mortgaged property.

In May 1904, Richard Norris of the Norris Entertainment Company met with Cervera and convinced him to return to St. Louis. The city was hosting that year's world's fair, titled the Louisiana Purchase Exposition, and Norris wanted Cervera to provide entertainment, not within the fair itself, but in a $25,000 bullring Norris was building just outside the fair. Norris would take care of advertising and secure necessary permits and permission from the city. Cervera need only bring the bulls and the bullfighters. After settling on financials, Cervera agreed, and he, his wife and some fifteen matadors and associated staff members boarded a train from Juárez to St. Louis. Among those to make the trip was the "American Matador" Carleton Bass, whom Cervera felt would appeal to local audiences.

As explained in newspapers, the first bullfight was to take place on June 5 and would be part of the Spanish cultural exposition, although it is unclear if Spain endorsed the event. Advertisements claimed that the bullfighters would perform the traditional violent practice of the sport, with Norris promising that local authorities had given their approval. Some seven thousand curious Americans bought tickets to the event, paying upward of one dollar apiece.

To the disappointment of those seeking to learn more about the blood sport—but fortunately for the bulls—the governments of Missouri and St. Louis were sympathetic to the progressive agenda, and they did not want to discredit the city during the world's fair. (The same month the bullfight was to take place, St. Louis police raided and shut down a roulette parlor run by R.C. Pate because it violated local gambling laws.) The president of the Humane Society, James Brown, telegraphed the governor of Missouri shortly before the event was to take place and asked him to stop "the barbarous, cruel, bloodthirsty, degrading, and demoralizing practice known as 'Spanish bull fighting.'"[125] Brown cited recent legislation banning bullfighting and bullbaiting in the state of Missouri and argued that the world's fair did not provide an exemption. The governor responded by writing a letter personally banning the event. Local Humane Society members put similar pressure on the city and county governments, leading them to also issue an injunction.

Not wanting to part with their profit, it seems that Cervera and Norris decided to carry through with the event. Instead of fighting bulls, they would imitate Buffalo Bill and hold a Wild West show without informing the crowd of the change. They commissioned the Cummings Wild West Show, which was performing at the world's fair, to open the performance. When the event commenced at 3:00 p.m. and a group of Indians and rough riders filed into the arena, the audience greeted them with boos and shouts of "Where's the bull? We want to see the bull!"[126] An actor playing Sitting Bull was met with chants of "We want a bull, not a Sitting Bull."[127] Some spectators, believing that they had been tricked, began throwing bottles into the arena, and one person threw a chair.

Apparently bowing to the pressure from the crowd, Cervera brought out his toreadors and was prepared to have them fight, but before he could unleash the bulls, the sheriff of St. Louis County entered the arena, placed the toreadors under arrest and read the governor's proclamation banning the event. The crowd grew livid at the development and demanded their money back. Norris apologized to the crowd and told them that he could not refund their money. After all, it was not his fault that the performance was canceled.

At this point, the audience cried, "Mob the sheriff!" leaped over the walls into the arena and started attacking the police.[128] Some among the mob suspected that the whole thing had been a ruse to rob them of their money, so a portion of the crowd broke off and began chasing Norris and the bullfighters. Some of the toreadors took refuge in the box office. Cervera fled to the nearby home where he and his wife were staying.

While Cervera was hiding, spectators "smashed seats and every other smashable thing in the arena." Someone lit a fire in a hay loft in the stables, prompting "great cheers from the thousands of spectators."[129] A second fire was set on the other side of the arena, spreading rapidly. Whether to save the animals or to generate even more chaos, a group of men opened the pens holding the bulls and horses. Others took to throwing bottles and chairs at the animals. Perhaps realizing the direction things were headed, the animals immediately ran out of the arena and headed for the hills. Fire companies from the world's fair arrived on the scene soon thereafter, but instead of putting out the fire, they wetted down the adjacent fair buildings to prevent them from catching fire. This left the bullring to burn down to "a heap of smoldering ashes."[130]

Police detained Norris, Cervera and their bullfighters following the tumult on charges of violating the anti-bullfighting statute and inciting a riot. The men insisted that they had no plans to harm the bulls, and they argued that they had no reason to start a riot. Considering that no bullfighting had actually taken place and there was no evidence that the bullfighters took part in the riot, the police dropped the charges and released the men.

Although they avoided arrest, the bullfighters were in a foreign country, they had yet to be paid and with the bullring burned down, they had no source of future revenue. This left the performers and crew with no job

MOB BURNS BULLFIGHT AMPHITHEATER WHEN MONEY IS NOT RETURNED AFTER OFFICERS PREVENT CONTEST

SHOWING THE CROWD THAT SURROUNDED THE OFFICE OF THE AMUSEMENT COMPANY FOLLOWING THE ANNOUNCEMENT THAT THE BULLFIGHT HAD BEEN DECLARED OFF.

After authorities canceled the bullfighting exhibition, a disappointed audience burned the amphitheater to the ground, leading police to arrest Cervera, his bullfighters and promoter Richard Norris. Norris would later protest his arrest, accuse members of the Humane Society of inciting the crowd and threaten to sue the city for $500,000. *From the* St. Louis Republic, *June 6, 1904.*

and no money to get home. Members of the troupe commissioned the Irish "American Matador" Bass to ask Cervera to talk to Norris and demand that he give them the money they were owed. The discussion between Bass and Cervera did not go well. The two men started arguing, and after an apparent slight, they drew pistols on each other, but before either could fire, onlookers separated the two. Cervera huffingly agreed to speak with Norris about paying the performers.

A few hours later, around 10:30 p.m., Cervera burst into his matadors' hotel room and told them that he was able to secure $200 from Norris. This was only enough to pay for train tickets to San Antonio, so Bass, who had been lounging on a nearby chair, stood up and demanded that Cervera give them all the pay they were owed. He went further and accused Cervera of

THIS DIAGRAM ILLUSTRATES BASS'
VERSION OF THE SHOOTING OF CERVERA

"B," Bass; "C," Cervera.

Artist depiction of Bass shooting Cervera. *From the* St. Louis Post-Dispatch, *June 9, 1904.*

pocketing some of the money Norris had intended for the bullfighters, a valid charge considering that at that moment Cervera's wife was on a shopping spree. Cervera took offense to the accusation, took a butcher knife from his belt and headed in Bass's direction, saying, "I'll fix you."[131] In response, Bass fell back on a bed behind him to increase distance, drew his pistol and fired, sending a bullet into Cervera's torso. The wounded matador cried, "I'm shot," and he fell to the floor dead.[132]

Police rushed to the room soon thereafter and asked what happened. All the bullfighters, including Cervera's close friend Mariano Leglera, gave the same version of events, exonerating Bass and saying that he had acted in self-defense. Authorities still arrested Bass for homicide and held him in jail until he could face a coroner's jury. When this happened a few days later, the jury accepted Bass's version of events and ordered that he be freed.

The riot outside the world's fair and the murder in its aftermath garnered headlines throughout the United States, making Bass temporarily famous.

One newspaper called him the "Matador of Matadors."[133] Hoping to capitalize on this notoriety and with Cervera dead, Bass took charge of the bullfighting troupe and made a deal with the owner of the Delmar Gardens to host a bullfight. Considering that the Delmar Gardens were within the St. Louis city limits, it is unclear how Bass expected to get around the laws banning bullfighting. Perhaps he hoped that after the riot, the police might be less willing to break up future events. Or that they might ignore the bullfight if it took place away from the world's fair at a smaller venue.

Cervera's widow, Marian Abell Cervera, grew livid upon learning of Bass's plans. She felt that Bass had killed her husband out of jealousy and that he and the other bullfighters had conspired to lie that her husband had approached Bass with a knife. Abell Cervera initially resigned herself to bringing her husband's body to Baltimore for burial, but after learning about the proposed show at the Delmar Gardens, she determined to avenge her husband through legal means, proclaiming, "That is now my only object in life."[134] She returned to St. Louis, went to the local police and demanded they shut down the exhibition.

With "a posse of deputy sheriffs at her back," Abell Cervera arrived at the Delmar Gardens just as Bass was preparing to battle a bull in front of an audience of hundreds.[135] She then marched into the ring and told Bass that if any harm came to the animals, he would be arrested. Not wanting to return to jail but fearing another riot if he refused to perform, Bass decided to put on a show where he would tease his bull opponent and sashay out of its way of when it charged but use no swords or barbs. Unfortunately for the Irish bullfighter, this routine only accomplished enraging the bull, and the frantic animal chased Bass out of the arena to the boos of a disgusted audience.

Bass and his crew tried to put on another performance shortly thereafter, but Abell Cervera once again showed up, this time taking a seat in the front row. When Bass entered the arena, the bullfighter's widow stood up and held up a life-size lithograph of her husband, prompting Bass to drop his sword and walk out of the arena. Bass attempted to secure additional venues for his bullfights, but Abell Cervera began following him around dressed in black, making sure that no one did business with the man whom she felt had murdered her husband. Bass supposedly exclaimed, "Those awful eyes! Everywhere I see them—night and day they haunt me, always threatening death."[136]

Bass grew despondent. According to one newspaper, "He had hopes of revivifying bull fighting in spite of opposition, but with Senora Cervera

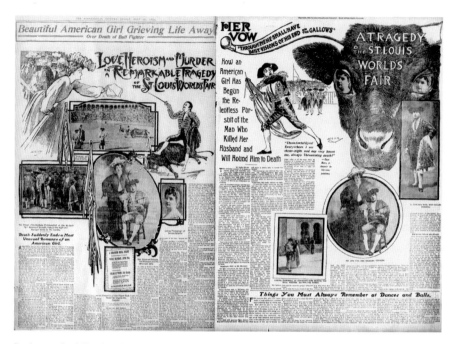

In the weeks following the murder, newspapers carried full-page sensationalist articles detailing Marian Abell Cervera's attempts to "avenge" her husband. *From the* Minneapolis Tribune, *July 17, 1904, and the* San Francisco Examiner, *August 7, 1904.*

as his nemesis he acknowledges himself beaten."[137] Bass left St. Louis and attempted to stage a few small shows in Texas a few months later, but police shut many of them down. Defeated, and with his heart no longer in it, Bass decided to retire from bullfighting the following year and returned to Ireland.

Interestingly, even with Bass gone, Abell Cervera continued to sabotage bullfighting programs in St. Louis, including a series of exhibitions planned by French bullfighter Felix Robert. Robert had recently performed as a bullfighter in Juárez, but it is unclear if he had come to St. Louis with Cervera or if he had simply arrived in the city hoping to fill the bullfighting gap left by Cervera's death and Bass's departure. Whatever the case, it appears that Robert hired many of Cervera's unemployed bullfighters to serve in his exhibition, which was set to begin on September 4. Hoping to avoid the legal problems his predecessors had faced, Robert spoke with newspapers and stated explicitly that "Ze bool is in no dangair whatevair" in his events.[138] Instead, he and his troupe would be the only ones in harm's way.

Prior to the first event, Abell Cervera confronted Robert and threatened to have the county shut him down. Robert mocked her and replied that "the county had been 'fixed' so that there would be no interference with the fights."[139] Abell Cervera responded by seeking the assistance of the local Humane Society, forming an interesting alliance, considering that it had been the Humane Society that had coordinated the effort to shut down her husband's bullfight in the first place. Together, the unlikely allies started a letter writing campaign to local politicians, and Abell Cervera even personally traveled to the Missouri state capitol to speak to the governor about shutting down Robert's shows. The governor responded by ordering the St. Louis sheriff to attend the fights, although he told him not to act unless Robert harmed an animal in violation of the law.

Some two thousand people showed up to the fight on September 4, but after seeing that the police were in attendance, few bought tickets, fearing that the event would be shut down and they would lose their money. This prompted Robert to promise that anyone who bought a ticket would receive their money back if the show did not take place, encouraging those outside to enter the arena. When Robert then ordered that the bulls be released to start the show, none came out. Abell Cervera, dressed in black from head to toe, had taken a position at the gate to the bullpen and closed it every time an attendant opened it. Eventually the widow gave up, but she then took to leveling insults at the matadors as they made their way into the arena.

Despite the efforts of Abell Cervera and the Humane Society, the insults and the presence of the police did not phase the matadors, who carried out their program with few problems. As promised, Robert and his toreadors taunted the bulls with their flags, sashayed out of the way when the animals charged and jumped into stalls whenever the bulls grew agitated. Robert spiced up things by performing hand stands and chair tricks whenever bulls charged him, and to sell the event as an educational exhibition, he used props to demonstrate how matadors killed bulls in traditional bullfights. Everything went so well that Robert put on four events over the next five days, and he announced plans for additional shows in the coming weeks.

Unfortunately for Robert and his bullfighters, the Humane Society convinced Missouri attorney general Edward Crow to ask the Clayton Circuit Court for an injunction preventing these future fights. Crow argued that despite Robert's theatrics, his shows still constituted bullfighting and bullbaiting and were "contrary to good morals and public peace and constitutes a continuing violation of the law."[140] He also reminded the court that a previous bullfight had led to a riot.

While waiting for the injunction, the prosecuting attorney of St. Louis charged Robert, his bullfighters and the men who owned the location where they had held their exhibitions with misdemeanor charges of bullfighting and bullbaiting. The toreadors went to trial on September 16, 1904, and prosecutors called up multiple officers of the Humane Society to testify that what Robert had put on was a bullfight. Prosecutors also called up Abell Cervera, but she did not show up, prompting officers to retrieve her.

When Abell Cervera eventually arrived, she was once again wearing all black, but this time she carried a cane. When she walked by Robert to take the stand, the two began arguing in Spanish, leading Abell Cervera to unsheathe a dagger hidden in the end of the cane, which she then attempted to use to stab the matador. According to one newspaper, "Roberts [sic] saved himself by a quick motion of his hand brushing aside the cane with a dexterity attained in the arena."[141] Undeterred, Abell Cervera fled the courtroom, remarking, "I'll get even with him yet."[142] It is unclear if the outburst affected the trial's outcome, but the judge ultimately sided with the bullfighters and dismissed the injunction and misdemeanor charges.

Two days later, Robert put an ad in the *St. Louis Post Dispatch* announcing, "Bull Fight Today: Our Case Sustained by the Courts."[143] The victory was short-lived. Upon learning about the court's decision, Governor Dockery issued an executive order banning any future exhibitions put on by Robert.

The governor's order brought an end to bullfighting in St. Louis and prompted Robert and his bullfighters to take the Mississippi south to New Orleans in the hopes of putting on a bullfight there. The executive order also seems to have ended Abell Cervera's career as an animal rights activist, as she does not appear to have been involved in any future Humane Society efforts. Even without her, the Humane Society and the American Society for the Prevention of Cruelty to Animals were able to convince the mayor of New Orleans to deny Robert a permit to hold bullfighting exhibitions in his city. His plans to bring bullfighting to the United States dashed, Robert returned to Juárez, where he would soon become one of the most prominent exhibitionists in the border city.

According to one newspaper, at least one bullfighter remained in St. Louis after the end of the world's fair: Manuel Cervera's ghost. As reported by the *St. Louis Post Dispatch Sun*, multiple people who passed by the house where Cervera stayed while in St. Louis would sometimes see the deceased bullfighter standing in the upstairs window. Strange sounds emanated from the house, and at least one person claimed to hear the toreador's song from *Carmen*. More chilling, when a searchlight set up for the fair flashed across the green house, the light would bend into a skull shape. Thrill-seeking children ignored the "No Trespassing" sign on the door to try to get a closer glimpse inside. An article reporting on the phenomenon noted that "Cervera came to St. Louis last May, brought from Mexico by the prospect of shining in the limelight of publicity as the greatest matador in the world." Instead, his ambitions aroused his madness, leading to his death, and now "Cervera's spirit haunts the scene of his downfall and death, striving vainly to get back the glory that is departed forever."[144]

CHAPTER 6

WHEN THE BUFFALO FOUGHT THE BULL

The deadening sound of skulls smashing against each other echoed across the Juárez bullring. The year was 1907, and an American bison and a Mexican bull had just collided head on. Promoters had brought the two animals together with dual purposes. They wanted to see which of the beasts was tougher, and they wanted to make money. Having sold ten thousand tickets to the event, the promoters had accomplished the latter goal. The only thing that remained, then, was to see whether the buffalo or the bull would be the first to fall.

The mastermind behind the fight was rancher James "Scotty" Philip. Although he would later become synonymous with the American West, Philip was of Scottish birth. In 1874, at the age of fifteen, he and a group of his fellow Scotsmen immigrated to the United States, where they founded the ranching town of Victoria, Kansas. Things did not go well for the new arrivals. Instead of raising cattle as they had intended, many of the young immigrants took to drinking and playing sports all day. Money soon ran out, and most of the Scotsmen packed their bags and returned to their homeland.

Not Philip. He went in search of gold. In 1874, George Armstrong Custer and the Seventh U.S. Cavalry discovered gold on Sioux territory in the Black Hills of South Dakota. Although it was federally recognized Indian land, white miners flooded into the Black Hills to make their fortunes, and towns like the infamous Deadwood soon sprang up to accommodate the new arrivals. The Sioux fought back against the violation of their territory, but the U.S. Army defeated them and forced them to accept smaller allotments of land as reservations.

Scotty Philip. *South Dakota State Historical Society.*

Philip would make his home on one of these Sioux reservations. Among the first to arrive in the Black Hills, Philip tried mining, but circumstance kept him from profiting in the endeavor. So Scotty—nicknamed for his Scottish ancestry—returned to herding cattle and soon became one of the wealthiest ranchers in the Dakotas. His success owed, in part, to Sarah Larribee, an American Indian woman whom Philip had wed while living in Kansas. Larribee's Indian ancestry allowed Philip to pasture his herd on Sioux land, something prohibited to whites without Indian relatives. Philip grew rich off this territorial monopoly, remaining on the Sioux reservation until the U.S. government opened the land to white settlers in 1898. In response to the new competition, Philip purchased a considerable amount of pastureland near the town of Fort Pierre and relocated his livestock.

By 1898, Philip's herd included not just cattle but also buffalo. American bison—more commonly referred to as buffalo—are 700- to 2,800-pound mammals native to North America. Herbivores, buffalo are rarely aggressive, using their horns only when necessary to fend off bears and mating rivals. Buffalo historically ranged across the North American Plains from Alaska to northern Mexico, where they formed the basis of Plains Indian society. Their meat provided sustenance, and Indians used buffalo hides as clothing, teepees and trade goods. Because buffalo were so important to native culture, Indians fostered buffalo growth by periodically burning the plains to create pastureland. With this help, the American bison population grew to nearly 30 million head by AD 1500.

By the time Philip acquired land near Fort Pierre in 1898, the buffalo population had dropped to less than 1,000. The animal had become a favorite target of American hunters, who had moved onto the plains in the mid-nineteenth century. Part of the westward expansion of white settlers from the burgeoning United States, these hunters followed the railroad, shooting upward of 100,000 buffalo per day for meat to feed railroad workers and for hides for clothing, international trade and industrial use. Using high-powered rifles that could drop an animal at one thousand yards, hunters also killed for no other reason than to hurt the Plains Indians, who depended on buffalo for survival. By 1880, hunting, along with the introduction of competing species and bovine diseases, had brought bison to the verge of extinction.

Scotty Philip developed an affinity for buffalo while living on the Sioux reservation in the Dakotas. Each year, he would witness herds crossing the plains during their seasonal migration only to see them return the following year fewer in number. Admiring the buffalo's majesty and tranquil nature, Philip decided to do something before hunters could eradicate the animal. He purchased bison from a neighbor who had rescued calves during a buffalo hunt and began raising the animals on his property near Fort Pierre. By 1907, Philip's bison herd had grown to some one thousand head, making his ranch home to more buffalo than the rest of the world combined.

Philip's efforts, an end to the West's Indian Wars and Buffalo Bill's Wild West Show—which featured American bison—made the United States sympathetic to the plight of the buffalo. By 1905, the American public was clamoring for the government to create reserves for the endangered animals. With the support of naturalist President Theodore Roosevelt, the people of United States unofficially adopted the buffalo as one of the nation's mascots. Americans grew proud and protective of the animal that they had almost brought to extinction. Philip catered to the renewed interest by selling buffalo from his ranch to parks, zoos and circuses.

This pride would lead Scotty to match one of his animals against a Mexican bull. According to one version of the story, when a group of Mexican diplomats visited Scotty's ranch in Fort Pierre and saw their first bison, they began to mock the animal for its slow and lumbering nature. Philip took offense to their jests and boasted that his buffalo were tougher than any fighting bulls in Mexico. He would even prove it by setting up a fight between the two animals. Another story says that Philip was visiting Texas when he overheard some Juárez men bragging about how tough their animals were; Philip wanted to show that his American animals were tougher. Yet another version holds that Scotty came up with the plan while drinking in a bar on Christmas. Whichever story is true, Philip wanted to show that American bison deserved respect.

Philip had the buffalo and the desire to put on the fight, but he did not have a Mexican fighting bull or even a place for the combat to take place, as animal cruelty laws and the ASPCA would not allow such a thing to occur on American soil. Fortunately—or unfortunately, from the animals' perspective—Philip's friend Bob Yokum had cousins in El Paso who could put the rancher in contact with the manager of the Plaza de Toros bullring

Philip's bison graze in South Dakota. Before the arrival of European and American hunters, an estimated 29 million plains bison ranged from the southern Canadian prairies to northern Mexico. *South Dakota State Historical Society.*

in Juárez. Bullfighting was legal in the city, and its location just across the border from El Paso meant that Philip could take the buffalo there by train.

Felix Robert managed the Plaza de Toros bullring in Juárez. Short, tan and almost always wearing a bright, wide smile, Robert was a former matador from France. Being a Frenchman in a trade usually dominated by Spaniards distinguished Robert from other bullfighters, as did his eclectic bullfighting techniques. Like traditional Spanish matadors, Robert enticed a bull with a cape, sashayed out of the way when charged, planted barbs into the passing animal's shoulders and finished the bull with a sword to the heart. What made Robert unique was his incorporation of French bull-leaping techniques: he would often carry a pole into the bullring with him, which he would use to vault over a charging bull. Robert's prowess earned praise from no less than the queen of Spain herself, a fact that the matador was always eager to share.

Although a praiseworthy bullfighter, as a manager Robert frequently put on awful bullfights. According to newspapers, the Plaza de Toros was less a bullring and more a butcher shop. Robert employed poorly trained, slovenly matadors who lumbered about the ring, displaying none of the artistry seen in bullfights in Spain. His bulls were scrawny, mangy and poorly bred. During bullfights, matadors clumsily stabbed at the pathetic animals, causing unnecessary pain and blood loss. Things were not much better for the bullfighters. Robert's matadors often found themselves punctured by a bull's horn, and there had been multiple human deaths in the Plaza de Toros. Just a year before, Robert had to cut short a tour in Tijuana because Americans had grown tired of the poor state of his bullfights, and considering that things were not going much better in Juárez, it remained possible that he would soon have to close up shop there as well.

Considering this sorry state of affairs, when Yokum's cousin approached Robert with Philip's idea for a different sort of animal fight, the matador jumped at the opportunity. They made a deal: if the buffalo lost, the South Dakota men would bear all the expense of the fight; if the buffalo won, Robert would pay the American's expenses and Philip would receive a portion of the gate receipts.

Robert scheduled the event for Sunday, January 27, 1907, telegrammed Philip and set out to find a suitable bull. The usual scrawny bovines that he used in his bullring would not do for such a large event. He needed a true Mexican fighting bull, the kind that possess an unnatural aggression due to hundreds of years of selective breeding. It seems that Robert found such an animal. Newspapers differ on the bull's origins—some saying that it hailed from Chihuahua and others Durango—but most agree that Robert found an excellent specimen that exceeded one thousand pounds and looked nothing like the cheap animals usually on display in his shows.

Now that he had a date and location, Philip scoured his herd for a buffalo to ship to Juárez. After careful consideration, he whittled his selection down to two animals. One was eight-year-old alpha male Pierre—named after Fort Pierre—who weighed nearly a ton and was among the largest in the herd. Unsure if Pierre's size would be a detriment in a fight with a fast-moving bull, Philip also considered a smaller but faster four-year-old male whom he called Pierre Jr. Unable to pick between the two animals and fearing that an injury might derail the whole operation, Philip took both, herding the bison on to a specially outfitted train car for the journey south. Bob Yokum and ranch hand Eb Jones joined Philip on the trip.

Just as the train prepared to depart in early January 1907, a massive snowstorm hit Fort Pierre, threatening to freeze Philip's cattle herds. Although he longed to see his buffalo compete, Philip decided that he needed to stay in Fort Pierre to care for his livestock. In his stead, he sent his twenty-seven-year-old nephew, George Philip. Although levelheaded and intelligent, George had less experience working with bison, having spent much of the last decade attending law school.

After a series of delays on the long train ride, George, Jones, Yokum and the buffalo arrived in Juárez on the morning of January 27, the day of the fight. Knowing that the animals would be in poor shape from being cooped up in the train for the past week, George hoped to delay the showdown with the bull. The circulars scattered throughout the town, the large crowd gathered at the Plaza de Toros and Felix Robert's actions quickly informed him of the impossibility of this plan. With crowds already piling into the Plaza de Toros, Robert had his men offload the buffalo and bring them to the bullring before the men from the Dakotas even exited the train. By the time George Philip and his companions made their way to the bullring to meet Robert, attendants were already prepping the buffalo to fight.

When George met Robert, then, the only thing left to do was to decide which of the two buffalo would fight. George settled on eight-year-old Pierre. Although he did not write down his thought process, it is possible that George saw Robert's chosen fighting bull and realized that even speedy Pierre Jr. would be unable to outrun its horns. Pierre's size advantage, on the other hand, might make a difference in the fight.

Both animals had fans in the audience. Because Robert had advertised the fight in both the United States and Mexico, the crowd was evenly divided between Americans and Mexicans. This would be the first visit to a bullring for most of the Americans, many of whom had come only to support the United States–born Pierre. It would also be their last time in a bullring. When the day opened with traditional bullfights, many Americans grew sick when they saw Robert's inept bullfighters awkwardly slaughter three bulls (an ironic reaction from spectators there to witness two animals fight to the death). When one bull chased a matador over a fence, the Americans cheered, mocked bullfighting as a sport and grumbled that it was time to get on with the main event.

Whether it was the American revulsion to their sport or sympathy for the Mexico-born bull, the Mexicans in the Plaza de Toros rooted against the buffalo. It is possible that some in the crowd saw the contest in nationalistic terms. In 1907, Mexico was on the precipice of revolution, owing, in part, to Mexican president Porfirio Díaz's pro-American policies: he allowed United States companies to exploit Mexican workers and permitted the sale of huge swathes of land in Mexico to private American citizens. Some in the crowd had probably been alive when the United States defeated Mexico in the Mexican-American War and annexed half of their country. To many Mexicans, the United States was a bully, providing ammunition to cheer the Mexican bull to take down one of America's symbols.

The chances of this happening looked good when fight time arrived. When the bullring's gates opened, Pierre lumbered through them as if he had not a care in the world. He showed no reaction to the crowd, sauntered to the center of the ring and just stood there, looking more like a statue than a dangerous animal. Although his size amazed those who had never seen a buffalo before, Pierre's lethargy had many in the crowd laughing. George Philip was not among them. He realized too late that Pierre had an injured knee, likely incurred while the animal kicked the side of his train car on the way to Juárez. The buffalo would have to fight hurt.

On the contrary, the bull that Robert had chosen was at full health and looked menacing when he stormed out of his pen into the arena. Without a moment of hesitation, the bovine set his sights on Pierre, dropped his horns, snorted and charged, aiming for the buffalo's exposed side. Pierre just stood there, perpendicular to the bull, looking blissfully unaware that a dangerous animal was preparing to imbed its horns in his side. To those in attendance, it looked like the buffalo was about to go down.

He was not. When the charging bull came within a few feet of Pierre, the buffalo pivoted toward the incomer, swung out his rear legs, lowered his head and drove it into the bull's forehead. The collision of the two animals' thick skulls produced an awful, sickening thud that reverberated throughout the arena, silencing the crowd. Newspapers reported that the sound echoed for blocks.

The bull had just received a harsh lesson in bison ethology. Whereas bulls use forward momentum and their hind legs to drive into opponents, buffalo rely on gravity and their front legs for power. They kick out their small hindquarters and allow gravity and their foreleg muscles to ram their dense skull and horns. They do not need to run to build momentum and can turn on a dime. The bull had been running not toward a defenseless opponent, but rather one that was fully prepared to fight.

The head-on impact dazed both animals. It seems that the bull was the first to recover from the blow because he circled Pierre and went to gore him a second time. Again, the buffalo turned at the last second and met his opponent head on. The bull's third charge met this same fate. The repeated blows finally began to affect both animals. Owing to concussion, his injured knee or a combination of the two, Pierre stumbled, lost his footing and collapsed. Fortunately for the buffalo, the bull did not attempt to gore his downed opponent, likely because he, too, was stunned. Refusing to let the match end so soon, the crowd grew angry and began to boo, forcing Robert to order an attendant into the ring to goad the buffalo into attacking the bull.

Pierre and the bull meet head on. Newspapers would later claim that the sound of the collision could be heard for blocks. *El Paso Public Library.*

The attendant crept into the arena clutching a long metal pole, which he used to poke Pierre's side. In response, the buffalo angrily rose to his feet, but instead of rushing his bovine opponent, he went after the guy who had just poked him with a stick. The sight of the charging one-ton animal sent the man running. He was able to make it to the side of the arena, but just as he was climbing over the top of the fence, one of Pierre's horns pierced his side. Thankfully for the attendant, he was able to drop to safety before the buffalo could do any serious damage.

The interlude with the attendant allowed the fighting bull to regain his composure, and as soon as Pierre turned his attention away from the fence, he found himself face to face with the bull. Once again, the animals collided, but this time they locked their horns and began twisting their heads in a struggle for domination. Horns dragged across flesh, opening wounds. Minutes passed before the two animals found separation.

Once free, the bloody and battered bull lined up for another charge. Again Pierre was ready. He reared up, and looking uninjured and displaying none of his previous lethargy, he met his opponent with his most forceful head butt yet. The bull collapsed. Realizing that he had been bested, the bovine quickly returned to his feet and fled to the other side of the bullring.

The sight of the retreating bull changed Pierre, instilling aggressiveness within him. No longer content to remain on the defensive, the large bison chased down his opponent and thrust his horns into his flesh. He did not stop at one blow, but instead opened a series of gashes. Accounts differ on the severity of the wounds, but one newspaper indicated that they were so substantial that blood covered the arena. Women fainted. Men turned their heads.

Eventually, the bull escaped Pierre's assault, fled to the other end of the arena and began "bellowing like a spoiled child."[145] He was unwilling and unable to fight any longer. Pierre snorted and stomped his feet defiantly but left the bull alone. The Americans in the audience cheered.

Although the bull had no fight left in him and the buffalo was the clear winner, Robert announced that the match was a draw because both animals were still alive; he operated under traditional bullfighting rules where victory meant the loser died in the ring. Many Americans, wanting Pierre declared the winner, grew angry over the decision. Mexicans in the crowd were similarly vexed. Used to seeing bullfights end in death, they wanted Robert to continue goading the animals to fight again.

The bullring manager came up with a way to keep both nationalities happy: he would put another bull in the arena with Pierre. None of his remaining bulls was as big and tough as the one that had just fought, but perhaps they would be able to capitalize on the bison's exhaustion and put up an entertaining fight. When Robert offered the Americans more money if he could carry through with his plan, George Philip replied, "Turn in all the damn bulls you wish, just so you give that buffalo room to turn around."[146]

When Robert's men loosed the second bull, it quickly became clear that he lacked the pedigree of his predecessor. When he charged, the now veteran Pierre head butted him three times in rapid succession, sending the bull fleeing around the ring. Robert brought in a third bull, but it, too, proved no match for the now aggressive Pierre. By the end of the afternoon, there were three bulls in the bullring doing their best to stay as far away from the buffalo as possible. After briefly chasing the animals, Pierre lay down in the center of the ring and took a nap.

When attendants opened the gates to signal the end of the fight, the bulls fled out of the arena as fast as they could. Pierre lazily made his way out to overwhelming cheers from the crowd. The buffalo had defeated not just one bull, but three, although the last two fights were such routs that many newspapers did not even bother to report on them.

A few traditional bullfighting fans were disappointed that none of the animals died in the combat, but most regarded the fight as a success. Americans crossed the border with stories to tell their neighbors. Cincinnati

The second and third bulls proved no match for Pierre. Some versions of the story say that Pierre's victory was more one-sided and that he actually defeated four bulls. *El Paso Public Library.*

resident W.S. Crawford was in attendance and took photographs. Telegraph cables carried his story and pictures to newspapers across the United States, and some of his photos would later be made into postcards. When Scotty Philip and the people of Fort Pierre opened their January 28 newspaper, an account of Pierre's victory greeted them.

George Philip and the men from Dakota were happy with their first day in Juárez. They made more money than the trip cost, and they redeemed the reputation of the American bison. Felix Robert had bet money on his bulls and lost, and he had promised the Americans to pay their transportation costs if they won—but he too was happy. Having sold out the Plaza de Toros for the first time in its history, ticket sales far outweighed his gambling losses.

Success inspired the French matador. Why settle for a single day of ticket sales when the buffalo could make him more money? Robert came up with a plan and proposed it to George Philip and his companions: he wanted his most famous (and only competent) matador, Rasulio Hernández, nicknamed El Cuco, to fight one of the bison. Known throughout Juárez as a kind and welcoming man, El Cuco was a stone-cold killer in the ring, having dispatched hundreds of bulls during his long career. Years later, George Philip remembered El Cuco as the "Babe Ruth of the Juarez bullring."[147] Mexicans would buy tickets to see their favorite matador redeem their nation after the bulls' poor showings. Americans would attend to cheer as their mascot made bullfighting look foolish.

George Philip agreed to Robert's plan because he believed that there was no way that his bison would lose. George even warned Robert that fighting an American bison would be much different than fighting a bull. Whereas cattle have only a thin layer of skin on their back to protect their spinal column and vital organs, buffalo have thick muscles and a dense fur coating. Because of this, matador barbs would be ineffective against a bison and would more than likely only upset the animal. Robert dismissed the American's concerns and bet $500 that El Cuco would kill his opponent. The ranchers accepted the bet, but only after warning Robert that there was a better chance that the buffalo would kill El Cuco than the matador would kill the buffalo. The Americans decided that Pierre Jr. should be the one to face the matador, feeling that it would be best to allow Pierre to recover from last Sunday's fight, as his leg injury had grown worse.

After the two parties agreed on money, Robert started advertising the upcoming event as a showdown between man and beast and set the bout for the following Sunday, February 3. Word of the fight spread quickly, sending Mexican elites and rich Americans to Juárez. Once again the Plaza de Toros sold out, netting Robert $8,000 in ticket sales. Even the governor of Chihuahua decided to attend the fight. Although he would not be traveling to Juárez, President Theodore Roosevelt learned of the showdown when the El Paso Humane Society asked him to contact the president of Mexico to put a stop to the contest. There is no evidence that the president entertained the request.

Sunday, February 3, 1907, was fight day. Robert hoped to open the event with three traditional bullfights, but things did not go as planned. After the first matador and his entourage made their way into the arena, attendants opened the gate holding the first bull. Nothing came out. After some cajoling, a bull emerged, but instead of heading in the direction of the matador, the animal ran to the closest fence and tried to climb out. In a cost-saving measure, Robert had used the same poor animal that Pierre had battered and bruised the week before. Apparently harboring memories of the encounter with the bison, the bull wanted to exit the arena as soon as possible. After failing to climb the fence, the animal began circling around the matador and refused to engage him. The fight with Pierre had reduced a prime fighting bull to seeing ghosts.

After the first bull refused to fight, Robert had a new matador and bull brought in. This second bull had also fought Pierre the week before, and he, too, refused to engage the bullfighter. Apparently Robert had not purchased any new bulls, as the third bull to enter the arena had also fought Pierre. He, too, circled the arena in fear. The crowd booed.

With the audience upset and the governor of Chihuahua growing angry, Robert prayed that the main event would make up for the disaster that had preceded it. It would not. After El Cuco walked into the bullring to much pomp and circumstance, the gate opened to allow Pierre Jr. to enter. He did so similarly to Pierre a week before, slowly and with little aggression. When El Cuco began waving his cape in the hopes of angering Pierre Jr., the animal just stared. Whereas fighting bulls charge when they see the motion of a matador cape, nature and breeding had not instilled such an instinct in bison.

Unlike Pierre, Pierre Jr. had never been an alpha male, had not faced combat in the ring and, having been raised on Scotty Philip's ranch, had nothing to fear from humans. He had no reason to go after the matador. To make the animal angry, then, El Cuco ordered a mounted picador to poke the buffalo with a metal pole. The prodding annoyed Pierre Jr. and the animal halfheartedly ran at El Cuco, but he did not seem interested in actually causing harm. El Cuco tried to wave his cape and make it look like he was in danger, but the audience was not buying it. They began to throw cushions into the ring and looked on the verge of rioting.

The buffalo fighting exhibition proved to be a disaster, but as seen in this advertisement, Felix Robert would try to put on a similar spectacle on at least two other occasions. *From the* Evening Telegram, *August 1, 1911.*

The display disgusted the already agitated governor of Chihuahua. To calm the crowd, he called Robert into his box and told him to call off the fight and refund everyone's money. In an attempt to placate the governor, El Cuco offered to at least execute the buffalo to satiate those in the crowd who had come for blood. The governor dismissed the offer and went further in his punishment. He fined Robert and his bullfighters $500 apiece and suspended El Cuco from bullfighting. As the crowd filed out of the arena, Robert and his staff returned their entrance money.

The Americans returned to El Paso for the night disappointed with the day but happy with the trip overall. Although they had missed out on seeing how an aggressive buffalo would fair against a matador, they had made plenty of money from the prior Sunday's fight, and they would be bringing home bragging rights to Fort Pierre. They even debated taking Pierre to Chihuahua City and Mexico City to put him up against the best fighting bulls Mexico had to offer but decided to instead net $200 by selling the two buffalo to an El Paso butcher, who planned to slaughter them and use their carcasses as an advertising stunt.

After sleeping overnight, the men returned to Juárez to retrieve their buffalo from the Plaza de Toros, where, according to George Philip, they found Robert sitting in his office surrounded by his matadors. The Frenchman was angry. He informed the Americans about the lost $8,000 in refunds and more in fines. To Robert, it had been the Americans' and Pierre Jr.'s unwillingness to fight that were to blame for the loss. He went further in his indictments, accusing Bob Yokum of flirting with the wife of one of his matadors.

To recoup his losses and restore his bullfighter's honor, Robert informed the Americans that he planned to sue them, and until trial, they had to wait in Juárez's notoriously dangerous jail to ensure that they did not skip out on their debt. George Philip and his companions grew angry. But before the Americans could consider leaving, they noticed that Robert's matadors had them surrounded, and each was wearing a shiny six-shooter on his belt. Unarmed, unwilling to spend what could be months in the Juárez jail and believing the matador might order his men to fire on them if they tried to escape, George Philip cut a deal with Robert. If the matador called off the lawsuit, they would allow him to keep Pierre. They would take Pierre Jr. to sell to the local butcher.

Although George's story may have happened just as he said, there are some discrepancies. Robert could be shady, and it would not be beyond him to demand the buffalo to cover expenses. However, he was a businessman, not a gunfighter, so it is unlikely that he intentionally had his men appear threatening.

Whatever happened, George, Bob Yokum and Eb Jones left El Paso with no bison when they boarded a train to Fort Pierre. Any disappointment they might have had over these circumstances was short-lived. When they arrived home, Scotty Philip and the people of Fort Pierre greeted them as heroes. Eb Jones continued to work on Scotty Philip's ranch, while Bob Yokum ran a general store in Fort Pierre. George Philip continued to help on his uncle's ranch and became a lawyer in Fort Pierre. Later in life, he wrote down the story of his time in Mexico in his memoirs.

The fate of Pierre is less clear, as inconsistencies between sources, and the fact that Robert no longer called the buffalo by its name, makes it impossible to follow him. Initially, it seemed that Robert planned to offset the blowback he received from the local Humane Society by announcing in April 1907 that he planned to donate a "five-year-old" buffalo to either the Humane Society or the City of El Paso. The age indicates that this was Pierre Jr., not Pierre, and considering the discrepancies in George Philip's version of events, this is certainly possible. However, it is more likely that the buffalo was Pierre and Robert had the age wrong. Whatever the case, after receiving the offer, city officials met with members of the Humane Society and accepted, announcing that they planned to display the animal in Washington Park for educational purposes. After learning of their plans, Robert rescinded his offer, fearing that the exhibit would serve as a "counter attraction to the bull fight."[148]

Instead, in May 1907, Robert showed the buffalo in the Juárez bullring but did not put the animal in harm's way, "on account of the fact that Manager Robert has other plans for the big buffalo."[149] The plan was that after the close of the bullfighting season, Robert was to bring Pierre to Mexico City, where on July 7 "the buffalo will be fought against a bull of Spanish fighting blood." Robert intended to bet $10,000 on the buffalo and said that he would take it to Madrid if it won.[150] The trip to Mexico City does not seem to have taken place in 1907, with one report indicating that Pierre was still nursing his injured leg.

By early the following year, Pierre seems finally to have recovered from his injury, and on April 10, 1908, Robert advertised that "war between the United States and Mexico will be declared on Sunday in the Juarez bull ring when a big American bison and a wild bull from the heart of the Sierra Madre will be pitted against each other."[151] He ordered a small wooden arena to be constructed within the bullring. This would prevent the animals from running away, as the bulls had done in the fight with Pierre the previous year, and would ensure that the battle was to the death.

El Paso newspapers offer little information on the fight, but a woman who witnessed the event later relayed what happened to George Philip when she met him in Fort Pierre. According to the woman, four bulls faced off against Pierre that day. None survived. Apparently, the wooden enclosure was well suited to the bison's method of head butting, while the bulls lacked space to build up momentum for their charges. One by one, the bulls were led down a small chute into the enclosure to battle Pierre. No longer resembling the timid, docile animal that entered the ring in January 1907, Pierre aggressively attacked each of his opponents, driving them to the side of the enclosure and then goring them with his short horns. According to the woman, Pierre hit one of his opponents so hard that the bull's lifeless body broke through the wooden enclosure and spilled out the other side. The only difference in the version reported in the *El Paso Times* is that the bull was the one who broke through the fence, smashing through to escape the buffalo.

The woman who spoke with George Philip said that following the victory, Robert planned to bring Pierre to Madrid to face off against the world's very best fighting bulls. This appears to be true, as in the summer of 1908, Robert planned a dual honeymoon/moneymaking trip to Spain. He first had the buffalo transferred from Juárez to El Paso. After the El Paso Port Authority and the chief of the Bureau of Animal Industry signed off, Robert shipped Pierre to Galveston, where it was then sent to New Orleans and finally Barcelona. Pierre seems to have fought at least once in Madrid, likely on September 13, but Spanish newspapers carried no details on the bout.

All indications are that Pierre remained in Spain for the rest of his life, as Robert returned to Juárez from Europe soon thereafter with no buffalo. In spite of this, the toreador would again turn to using buffalo in his shows in 1911, when he advertised another fight between a matador and buffalo in Salt Lake City. The results of the contest are unknown, but the bout involved neither El Cuco nor Pierre. A bull had shattered El Cuco's back years before, and the buffalo was from a local ranch.

CHAPTER 7

THE FURTHER ADVENTURES OF FELIX ROBERT
(PART I)

T he bout between Pierre and the bulls was not the only interspecies fight that Felix Robert staged on the Mexican side of the border. Indeed, Robert earned a reputation for presenting elaborate, sadistic fights between a variety of animals, and he more than any other would profit from the practice. For his actions, Robert faced his own battles with groups like the Humane Society and the American Society for the Prevention of Cruelty to Animals, which recruited American and Mexican media and politicians to bring down the fight empresario.

Robert's entry into the interspecies combat game came through bullfighting, a profession that appealed to him from a young age. Robert was born Pierre Cazenabe in Dax, Landes, in the southwest of France in 1868. His birthplace meant that Cazenabe was exposed to a different type of bullfighting than what was normally on display in Spain. Whereas Spanish matadors traditionally used capes to taunt bulls and then sidestepped out of the way when charged, matadors from southern France forwent capes and instead used poles to leap over charging bulls. To make things even more dramatic, they sometimes entered the bullring with their feet tied. With such daring, it is understandable that at fifteen Cazenabe fell in love with French bullfighting and spent the following twelve years learning the sport.

After doing things the French way early in life, Cazenabe traveled to Spain to learn traditional bullfighting, perhaps understanding that French bullfighters were not as well respected worldwide as their Spanish counterparts. To this end, he joined Manuel Carmona's elite bullfighter

Felix Robert and his bullfighters. Like many promoters of the time, Robert told contrasting extravagant stories about his past. Because of this, his age, birthplace and given name differ across sources. *El Paso Public Library.*

training program, where he learned how to taunt and execute bulls using traditional methods. Apparently, the Frenchman was an impressive student. Upon graduating, he became one of only twelve people in the world to hold a diploma from the program and the only foreign-born person to do so. At one point during his training, he even gained an audience with the queen, who was amazed by one of the Frenchman's performances. It was during his time in Spain that Cazenabe dropped his birth name and adopted the more unique-sounding Felix Robert as his *nom de combat.*

By the time Robert received his diploma, he had developed into an exceptional athlete. Although short in height, Robert weighed a stout 155 pounds, with dense muscle mass developed through training and recreational fencing. As one newspaper described him in 1904, "He has sturdy build of shoulders and calves and biceps hard as rock."[152] He was also handsome, "a small, dark man with even white teeth and a smile like a cherub."[153] When he first began bullfighting in Spain, Robert accentuated his appearance with a mustache, causing a commotion because no other bullfighter in the nation had worn a mustache for 250 years. He finally shaved it off to the approval of the Spanish public.

Robert also adopted a stereotypical bullfighting attitude. He liked to brag about his accomplishments. When he entered the ring, he often wore outfits worth thousands of dollars, something of which he made everyone aware because he developed an annoying habit of reminding everyone just how much he spent on things. This peacocking was at least partially a business tactic meant to show attendees where the cost of their tickets went, but Robert also seems to have taken pleasure in showing everyone just how exceptional he was. Robert's attitude also came from a deep love for his sport. He felt that bullfighting was an art and that its practitioners deserved as much respect as boxers, baseball players, painters and actors.

It was for this reason that Robert would spend much of his life trying to popularize his sport in his home country of France. In 1894, he tried to hold a bullfight in his hometown, but the minister of France, as part of a growing fraction of Europeans adopting stances against animal cruelty, ordered the event canceled. The police shut down the bullfight just as it was starting, causing the crowd to grow upset and begin rioting. In the ensuing chaos, a bull got loose from its enclosure. It escaped the arena and emerged just as parishioners were leaving mass at a neighboring church. The animal charged, but before he could harm anyone, Robert chased him down and killed him. The street became known as "Rue de Toro" for the toreador's impromptu performance.

In another instance, in Paris on June 5, 1900, a group of animal rights activists gathered outside the Duell Arena to protest an upcoming bullfight. They belonged to a growing animal rights movement in France and throughout the world, the members of which saw bullfighting as savage and inhumane and who were willing to take extreme measures to bring about its end. When the protestors saw a carriage bringing Robert and his fellow toreadors to the arena, one young man pulled out a pistol and shot at them, the initial bullet grazing Robert's cheek. A second shot would have ended his life had Robert not ducked his head just in time, sending the bullet into the cart driver instead. Robert then leaped from carriage, disarmed the shooter and began pummeling him in the face, leaving him with a broken jaw by the time police arrived.

Although Robert dreamed of broadening the appeal of bullfighting among his countrymen, by late 1900 he had realized that French public and government was soundly against the sport, so he left for the Americas.

He traveled to Mexico, where, like Manuel Cervera before him, he realized he could make a substantial profit putting on shows at the Plaza de Toros in Juárez for American tourists. Also like Cervera, he concluded in 1904 that "the United States is the best country in the world for making money."[154]

After Carleton Bass killed Cervera in 1904, Robert traveled to St. Louis to set up his own bullfighting exhibition outside the world's fair. It was there that Cervera's widow and the Humane Society had him arrested for bullfighting, and it was at the subsequent court hearing that Abell Cervera tried and failed to kill him. The charges of bullfighting failed to stick, but after the governor of Missouri ordered the exhibition shut down, Robert left the city. On the advice from the Humane Society and the Society for the Prevention of Cruelty to Animals, the mayor of New Orleans similarly banned Robert from performing in his city.

Forced out of the United States but recognizing that the American desire for blood sport meant money, Robert returned to Juárez. With Cervera's death, there was a vacancy in the Plaza de Toro's upcoming schedule, and so Robert leased the arena for a series of shows extending from Christmas Day 1904 to March 1905, the end of that year's bullfighting season. Unlike Cervera's sloppy performances, Robert's first year of shows was strictly professional. He brought in legitimate bullfighters from Spain to put on traditional bullfights, and he himself frequently fought in the ring to glowing praise, with the *El Paso Times* describing him as "the most popular of the matadors ever seen in Juarez."[155] The competing *El Paso Herald* also noted Robert's professionalism and said that he was making headway toward removing the bad impression Cervera and previous managers had given bullfighting.

Robert seems to have recognized from the start that a friendly relationship with the American press meant that reporters were more likely to frame his bullfights in a positive light. This, in turn, would draw larger audiences to attend his events and help him counter the influence of the growing animal rights movement, which had hampered his efforts to bring bullfighting to France and St. Louis. To this end, at the close of his first season in Juárez, Robert hosted six El Paso newspaper writers for a twelve-course banquet under an awning in the center of the Plaza de Toro's bullring. After dinner and wine, Robert made an imperceptible motion to one of his attendants, who loosed a Durango bull into the arena, which went straight for the diners. Most of the journalists ran for the fences, but one, Paul Johnson, teased the animal with a napkin, only to be tossed several feet in the air. Fortunately, Robert had had his men shave the animal's horns down, so they were incapable of inflicting any real damage. The stunt was taken in good humor by the El Paso press, and some became even more infatuated with the French matador than they had been before.

Indeed, one El Paso newspaper man, Hector McLean, was so enamored that he worked with the matador to write and translate a booklet titled *The Art of the Toreador* based, in part, on Robert's bullfighter's career. McLean had fallen in love with bullfighting after an April 2, 1905 incident in which a Kansas City tourist dared McLean to enter the Juárez bullring and fight a newly released bull. Apparently, McLean said, "I am game," jumped into the ring, stuck two bandoleros into the shoulder of the animal and scaled the walls to return to his seat. Newspapers the following week reported erroneously that he was "the first American who ever entered the Juarez bull ring."[156] Unfortunately, no copies of Robert and McLean's book survive today, with McLean having lost his personal copy within in a few years.

After his lease was up in Juárez, Robert moved to Tijuana, where he performed four shows in summer 1905. At first, the press in California held the matador in high regard, and Robert levied the positive attention to hobnob with American elites. For example, while in neighboring San Diego, he had the opportunity to have drinks with recently retired world heavyweight boxing champion and future "Great White Hope" Jim Jeffries, and the two discussed their respective sports.

He also took the opportunity to romance prospective partners. With the play *Carmen* still popular, the California press delighted in detailing a burgeoning romance between Robert and one the daughters of Luis Terrazas, former governor of Chihuahua and one of the wealthiest men in Mexico. While the matador almost certainly would have welcomed marrying into the powerful Terrazas family, the relationship does not seem to have evolved further, or it was entirely an invention of the California press in the first place.

Before long, the press in California moved away from publishing puff pieces about the bullfighter. As in France and St. Louis, there was a strong animal rights movement in California, and many residents disapproved of the bullfights across the border. For example, C.E. Van Loan of the *Los Angeles Examiner* found Robert's shows repugnant, especially when bulls gored the "pain-crazed horses," forcing them to go "galloping about with their inner mechanisms indecently exposed to the gaze of the morbidly curious."[157] Writers called out the matador for running a "bull con," and whenever they dictated Robert's words in the newspaper, they did so in an unflattering French accent.[158] The hostile articles and "fear of ridicule" made Robert much more hesitant to speak with the Los Angeles reporters than he had been those in El Paso.[159]

It is perhaps due to the unfriendly press that Robert returned to Juárez in September 1905 and leased the bullring for the next eight months, the entirety of the 1905–6 season. The Samaniego family may have awarded the contract because Robert performed a funeral show in honor of their patriarch, who died in October 1905. Whatever the case, the bullfighter seemed determined to up the ante from his previous stint in the city, and he began advertising that he would perform in the acrobatic French style during his second tour. He also claimed to have found even fiercer bulls, and he increased the number that would be killed each performance. He also took to performing parades in El Paso to advertise upcoming events.

Both El Paso newspapers reported positively on the bullfights throughout 1905 and into 1906, possibly influenced by the fact that rising attendance meant that Robert could pay for advertising in the periodicals. Indeed, Robert's shows accumulated enough capital for the Frenchman to purchase a home in El Paso on South Kansas Street. He also socialized with local elites in both El Paso and Juárez, and the El Paso City Council even allowed him to put on an educational exhibit north of the border. Things were going so well that after another summer stint in Tijuana, he once again leased the Juárez bullring for the 1906–7 season. By this time, Robert could afford to pay other bullfighters to perform in his stead, and so he announced that after a few shows at the beginning of the season, he would stop performing himself and focus entirely on management.

Robert's second full year as manager would not run as smoothly as his first. On November 17, in what was supposed to be one of his final performances, a bull tossed the French matador, inflicting moderate injuries. Matador Francisco Alonzo Paquiro, known as the Hebrew bullfighter, replaced Robert in the show, but the bull sent one of its horns through his left hip and carried "him about the ring, blood streaming from the wounds in the man's body."[160] The sight apparently sickened spectators and caused a few to faint, so the show was called after only two bulls, rather than the promised four.

Robert recovered from his injuries, but things grew worse for him when George Philip came to town with his two buffalo in early 1907. At the time, Robert had not yet stooped to putting on interspecies fights, so it is unclear why the matador accepted Philip's offer to pit one of his buffalo against a bull. Perhaps, as George Philip would later tell the story, Robert believed that his bulls were superior animals to buffalo, and he put on the show as a matter of pride. More likely he had reached the same conclusion as previous promoters: sensational events resulted in high ticket sales. Whatever the case, Robert's decision initially proved profitable. Although he placed a bet that his bulls would beat the American buffalo and lost, the event filled out the Plaza de Toros and netted Robert a substantial profit.

Unfortunately, he lost all those profits the following week when he tried to stage a bullfight between his best matador, El Cuco, and a buffalo. After the buffalo refused to engage or even acknowledge the matador, the governor of Chihuahua ordered Robert to return all ticket sales and pay a fine. Some sources claim that the governor even rescinded Robert's license to manage the Plaza de Toros. If this was true, the measure was only temporary, as Robert was putting on shows within a few weeks. In retrospect, a cessation of the bullfights might have been a good thing, because during an April 14, 1907 event, a particularly vicious bull "badly mangled and probably fatally injured" El Cuco.[161] Bulls gored two additional bullfighters at an event shortly thereafter.[162]

The biggest fallout from the buffalo fights was that it emboldened animal rights activists in El Paso. Prior to the bouts, the Humane Society of El Paso objected to the bullfights across the river in Mexico, but ultimately, its members seemed resigned to accepting that they could do nothing to stop the events in their sister republic. The attention brought by the buffalo exhibition seems to have changed this perspective. Not only did the Humane Society attempt to have local and national politicians put a stop to the buffalo bouts, but following the fights, they increasingly wrote to El Paso newspapers with criticisms of traditional bullfights. In response, the *El Paso Herald* became more antagonistic to Robert, and it increasingly focused on the cruelty done to the animals when reporting on bullfights. Newspapers outside the region also took to criticizing the events in the Juárez, especially how bulls frequently disemboweled the horses picadors rode in the bullring. For example, a report in the *St. Louis Globe-Democrat* held little sympathy for El Cuco after a bull broke his back, but it lamented that the bull also gored horses.

Robert tried to offset the criticism and show that he cared for animals by donating one of the buffalo to the Humane Society. Any goodwill he gained from the gesture was short-lived. After learning that the Humane Society planned to give the animal to the City of El Paso for display at Washington Park, Robert rescinded his offer, fearing that it would serve as a "counter attraction to the bull fight."[163]

In May 1907, the brutality of the Juárez bullring, and particularly the treatment of horses there, came to the attention of Minnie Maddern

Fiske, the most famous actress of the time and the vice-president of the International Humane Society. Fiske was an evangelistic progressive who believed that it was her duty as a famous actress to promote the arts and improve society in ways she deemed appropriate. Fiske was particularly passionate about the plight of animals, and she loved horses. Indeed, after she first learned about bullfighting, Fiske asked her friend Mark Twain to write a story condemning the practice. Twain responded with "A Horse's Tale," which appeared in two installments of *Harper's Magazine* in 1906. The story focuses on a thirteen-year-old girl and her horse, Soldier Boy. Through a series of events, the girl loses her horse, and it ends up in a bullring, where a bull disembowels it. The girl runs to the animal's rescue, only to also be killed by a charging bull.

On May 30, 1907, the El Paso playhouse, the Texas Grand, hosted a performance of *The New York Idea*, a comedy starring Fiske in which a group of New York women discuss matters of love, "the abominations of a loveless marriage" and the merits and deficiencies of divorce.[164] Fiske arrived in El Paso a few days before the play was scheduled, and one newspaper reported that she took the opportunity to take in a bullfight in Juárez and found it disgusting, particularly the way in which the bulls attacked the defenseless horses ridden by the picadors.

Considering that she had previously railed against the sport, it is more likely that Fiske did not actually attend a bullfight herself, but instead learned about the buffalo-bull fights and the death of the five horses in the previous month's show. It is also possible that Fiske first became aware of Robert's bullfights when reading a review of her play in the May 31, 1907 edition of the *El Paso Times*. The review, which called Fiske "America's greatest actress," appeared alongside a news clip about the matador El Gallo, who was set to appear in one of Robert's shows the following Sunday. El Gallo outshone Fiske's "greatest actress" appellation with the even more impressive descriptor "the best in the business."[165]

Whatever triggered her, Fiske grew "deeply grieved to learn of the complaisance with which one of our American cities treated the fact of the existence of bull fighting so near our own country" and made ending animal combat in Juárez one of her life goals.[166] She began coordinating with the El Paso Humane Society to find ways to undermine bullfighting economically. Recognizing that the spectacles along the border survived due to the patronage of Americans more than the people of Mexico, she implored parents, teachers and clergymen to use their influence to stop their friends and family from attending the fights.

Actress and activist Minnie Maddern Fiske. Fiske once said that President Theodore Roosevelt was a "bad example for boys" for going on a hunting trip. *Wikimedia Commons.*

Fiske also asked El Paso residents to do what they could to promote Mexican opposition to bullfighting. Displaying the type of progressive paternalism that was common at the time, she hoped to teach those south of the border "some slight lesson in the matter of humane education. I am sure there must be some humane people among the Mexicans if we can reach them."[167] She also "engaged in a quiet campaign to mold the opinions of the rising generation" of Mexican children by having allied Mexican school officials distribute Spanish-language versions of animal-friendly books such as *Black Beauty* and *Friend and Helper*.[168]

Fiske and the El Paso Humane Society's biggest tactic was to deny Robert the ability to advertise in El Paso. This included a letter writing campaign to the *El Paso Times* and the *El Paso Herald* asking the newspapers to no longer carry advertisements for bullfights in their papers and limit their coverage of events. The progressive groups believed that writing about the fights encouraged attendance and inspired new spectacles. This was not unreasonable, considering that a few weeks after the buffalo-bull fight, the El Paso Elks Lodge brought badgers from Mexico to a national meeting in Philadelphia with the intention of fighting them against local bulldogs. The El Paso men wanted "to show some genuine sport of the true southwestern variety."[169]

Although the *El Paso Times* did not respond to the Humane Society's pleas immediately, perhaps not being able to turn away the revenue, the *El Paso Herald* refused to renew Robert's advertising contract after it expired in May 1907. In addition, from that time forward, the *Herald* took an antagonistic stance toward bullfights and interspecies fights, either ignoring them or portraying them as savage. The newspaper also increasingly carried opinion pieces that denounced bullfighting, one of which noted that "cruelty begets cruelty and by tolerating the bullfights as a recognized amusement for El Pasoans, even though they be on foreign soil, across the Mexican boundary, we are condoning an institution whose influence is wholly bad, and whose product is savagery and immorality, pain and crime."[170]

Fiske and the El Paso Humane Society also pursued legal means to limit or end bullfighting across the border, calling on the El Paso City Council and Mayor Joseph U. Sweeney to pass legislation against Robert. On January 24, 1908, Humane Society–friendly members of the city council, led by Alderman Blumenthal, drove through legislation forbidding parades that promoted bullfighting or other acts of animal cruelty, claiming that a majority of El Paso residents supported such a law. Through an executive order, Mayor Sweeney made it illegal to pass out leaflets advertising upcoming fights.

The day after the legislation was announced, Robert wrote an incredibly tone-deaf letter to the *El Paso Times* imploring the people of El Paso to ask their councilmen to repeal the new laws. The letter, which Robert titled "I Accuse," contested Alderman Blumenthal's claim that the legislation was something most in El Paso wanted. Instead, Robert said, "I want the people of El Paso to know who are opposing the bull fights. They are a few women and the clergy. They are not only against the bull fighting, but they are against almost everything else. They do not want saloons, theaters, sport or recreation of any kind." He went further, stating, "They seem to think themselves self appointed dictators to everybody, very superior to the average human, and for this reason, take it upon themselves to lay our course of life. They take most people for fools and in need of guardians."[171]

Robert, on the other hand, felt that the people were "not in any great need of anyone to tell them what to do," and in what could be considered a deconstruction of the whole progressive movement, said that "there is a growing tendency in the rural districts of the United States to do away with all kinds of sport, saloons, recreation, etc....and to supply their places by the church."[172] He then compared the events in his bullring to that of the theater but claimed that his sports were morally superior to acting because they focused on bravery. Robert then personally called out Mrs. Fiske for starring in a play where the characters had sex outside of wedlock and chided the *El Paso Herald* for bowing to the whims of the progressives. He also criticized the paper for waiting until his advertising contract had run out before taking a stand.

In addition, Robert made an economic and legal argument against the recent legislation, claiming that his parades brought thousands of dollars to El Paso. Although he argued that the controversy only served as better advertisements for his events, Robert maintained that he wanted to fight the legislation because it violated the constitution and warned, "If I cannot distribute [pamphlets] lawfully, it will be a hard matter for any one else to do so." He also threatened, "I will also see to it that the ordinance regarding parades is observed by every circus that comes to town." He closed by saying that the American people "should not be dictated to by a few and that the American word 'Liberty' should not be lost sight of."[173]

Mayor Sweeney responded to Robert's treatise by saying, "Mr. Robert's exhibition is not courageous, manly or human. It is cowardly for a lot of savage men to get into the ring and torture a big dumb brute." He called the comparison to plays "a joke" and promised that while he was mayor, the legislation would be upheld. He also noted that "an exhibition of that kind would not be tolerated on this side of the Rio Grande"[174]

Fiske continued her fight, traveling to El Paso and Juárez in June 1908 to personally pass out circulars that denounced animal fighting and, in what was likely a personal attack on Robert, noted that "the Greatest Coward is he who treats with cruelty any helpless living thing." Her circulars called on American tourists to boycott the fights and asked Mexican politicians "in the name of humanity and decency cut out the bull fight from your program for Mexico."[175] While in Juárez, she thanked the *El Paso Herald* and reassured its editors that New York and Washington newspapers approved of its actions. She also personally donated a substantial sum of money to the Mexican Society for the Prevention of Cruelty to Animals. Although the effectiveness of Fiske's personal campaign is debatable, the *Herald's* decision not to advertise and the laws against parades and passing out billets seem to have led to a decline in attendance in the bullring in 1907 and 1908.

CHAPTER 8

THE FURTHER ADVENTURES OF FELIX ROBERT (PART II)

Robert responded to Fiske, the Humane Society and the ASPCA's attacks and the decreased ticket sales by abandoning his efforts to put on credible bullfights; he instead turned to staging increasingly bizarre, elaborate and dangerous stunts at his shows to drum up word of mouth and draw American crowds to Juárez. As one newspaper phrased the situation, audiences were "craving new sensations and fresh horrors of the ring."[176] Robert wanted to appease them. Indeed, the promoter staged multiple interspecies fights, and when he put on bullfights, he ensured that his performers either looked good when doing so or they faced legitimate danger.

Unfortunately, the exaggerated difficulty of these stunts led to accidents. In September 1907, for example, the matador Morenito Chico staged a show where he vaulted over a raging bull and then casually sat in a chair, from which he would attempt to stab the bull with bandilleros. The bull proved too fast for him. It charged and opened a wound in the matador's thigh and then tossed Chico over its head. In another fight, a bull threw matador Augustín Velasco from his feet, pierced his thigh as Velasco tried to stand up and then drove a horn "into Velasco's body, piercing the intestines and the liver."[177] In January 1908, Robert put on a show featuring Señorita Elvira Segobia and her troupe of female bullfighters, wherein one of the women sat in the center of the ring while another stood on her back awaiting a bull's charge. Although none of the female bullfighters was hurt, members of the crowd quickly realized that the women faced off against much tamer bulls than the men.

Robert also turned to additional interspecies fights involving large mammals to increase attendance. On April 30, 1908, at the end of the bullfighting season, Robert married Trinidad Ochoa, and the couple immediately set off for Europe for their honeymoon, touring France and Spain by automobile. However, Robert had an ulterior motive for their trip: it was at this point that Robert took the buffalo Pierre to Spain to fight, likely netting a substantial profit from the exhibition. The couple also visited Paris and parts of Africa, and during these stopovers, Robert made plans to have at least two old-world animals shipped to Juárez for interspecies fights.

In Africa, he paid $2,000, a figure he made public, to purchase "the fiercest tiger to be found" on the continent, which he arranged to have shipped to Juárez.[178] Tigers, of course, do not originate in Africa, and the animal that eventually arrived in Juárez was much smaller than a typical tiger. This was because the animal was, in fact, a leopard, which tops out at about two hundred pounds, compared to Bengal tigers, which can grow to more than six hundred pounds. In calling the leopard a tiger, Robert may have been intentionally masking the fact that he was purchasing a less physically impressive animal, but it is more likely that he was not being intentionally deceptive. In the popular conscience of the time, the delineation between one feline species and the next was not as clearly defined as it would later be, so whereas an expert might see a leopard as distinct from a tiger, the common man might call both a tiger.

News spread that Robert was importing a tiger, prompting J.B. Lawler, an African American part-time boxer and full-time elevator operator at the Orndorff Hotel in El Paso, to let it be known that he wanted to fight the animal, with the "novel plan of gaining a reputation or of getting killed." Like Billy Clarke before him, Lawler had been trying to secure a boxing match in El Paso, but owing to local laws, segregation in boxing and a lack of competition in the area, "There seems to be nothing doing in the genus homo line." The pugilist said that he had previously fought tigers and wanted only two short spears. He recognized that Robert was unlikely to put the animal up if it might die, so Lawler "guaranteed not to kill it unless to save his own life." Lawler promised, "I, Mr. Robert will consent for this tiger to meet me" and finished with, "The challenge is open and I hope he will accept it."[179] Robert never responded. The bullfighter apparently drew the line at putting a human in a cage with a leopard.

The week of October 11, 1908, Robert ran advertisements in the *El Paso Morning Times* for a "fight to the death" to take place between the "tiger" and a bull the following Sunday. The *Times* described the leopard as "a husky looking beast and from the way he continually milled around his cage he would tackle almost anything that came within reach, whether it be a wild bull or a Gatling gun." The newspaper promised that the upcoming event would be "the best program ever offered for the money" and implored its readers, "Don't miss this wonderful attraction."[180]

Likely because many newspapers had decided to no longer cover Robert's spectacles, little is known about the event. In spite of the lack of reporting and feeling that the "feature would prove a disappointment,"[181] the fight between the bull and leopard drew a "large crowd."[182] Robert had commissioned an iron sixteen-by-sixteen-foot cage constructed that was so small "neither animal could move about very easily."[183] The buffalo-bull fights had taught the matador that if given a large area to maneuver, the animals might not engage each other. He may also have heard stories about the previous fights between lions and bulls, wherein a large space allowed the bulls to build up momentum and dispatch the big cats with ease. To prevent the audience from getting upset over a tie and for betting purposes, Robert hired judges to rule on the fight.

When fight day came on October 18, 1908, the bull indeed found it difficult to maneuver in the small cage. This allowed the leopard to act first when it was introduced to the cage. As one newspaper described the scene, "The big cat, despite the handicap of weight and size, did his best to secure a hold on the bull." He jumped between the bull's horns multiple times in the hopes of taking the larger animal's back, so "he could bring his long, keen claws into play." Each time, the bull managed to shake off the cat before it could do serious damage and followed up with a charge. Four times the cat leaped out of the way and followed up with attacks of his own, inflicting deep scratches on the bull with its teeth and claws. However, the fifth time the bull charged, the leopard "failed to leap high enough and was crushed against the side of the cage." Unable to move, the leopard "fastened his teeth in the bull's nose and refused to be shaken loose."[184] The bull responded by stepping on the leopard.

A flap of flesh loosened from the bovine's face, but the bull did not cease the pressure and the two animals remained in their respective positions for long enough that the crowd grew upset with "half calling for the fight to be stopped, and the rest insisting that it be as advertised, to the death."[185] A portion of the audience even moved on the cage in the hopes of stopping the event, but Robert had his attendants drive them back, allowing the event to continue. Shortly thereafter, the bull, "maddened by the bites and scratches of the tiger...lowered his head and trampled his antagonist, pawed him and

Undated photograph of the Juárez bullring. It is difficult to make out what is happening in the image, but it appears to be a large feline, possibly the leopard, facing off against a bull. *University of Texas at El Paso Library Special Collections Department.*

dashed him against the sides of the cage. The tiger lay on his side in the ring, vainly struggling to get to its feet, and continue the already-lost fight for above five minutes, and was finally barred up in one end of the cage."[186] The leopard succumbed to his wounds. Some newspapers reported that the bull died as well, while others said he had no lasting damage and survived.

Despite pressure from animal rights organizations, a few newspapers reported on the event, with one calling it "a furious fight between two maddened beasts" that took spectators "back to memories of the dark days of Nero."[187] The news even made its way to Australia, although it had to compete for headlines with a tiger-bull fight put on in France.

The hype encouraged Robert to put on additional fights between large mammals. In December 1908, Robert reported that he was in negotiations with Hagenback's Circus of Hamburg, Germany, to purchase a four-year-old, 436-pound Bengal tiger to pit against a bull. Unlike the leopard, this was a true tiger, an apex predator, one of the deadliest animals in all of nature and much rarer in North America than even African lions. The animal arrived in Juárez on December 31, and three days later, Robert had the tiger wheeled into the arena and fed during that day's bullfighting show. He encouraged photographers to take pictures of the animal. Reporters noted that "the Prince of beasts was in no mood to be interviewed," although he appeared to be in fine condition.[188]

One of these pictures appeared in advertisements in the *El Paso Times* the following week, along with advertisements proclaiming, "There will take place the biggest event ever in this part of the continent."[189] Newspapers played up the upcoming bout by speculating on who would win and publishing questionable facts about tigers. One noted that the tiger's "method of attack is, usually, to spring on the back of the bull and literally tear him to pieces" and claimed that tigers kill about one thousand people annually in India.[190] Robert played into the hype by hiring former Rough Rider Ben McClannahan to serve as a referee. The attention worked. Robert managed to sell some 3,500 tickets, most sold to Americans.

The fight took place on January 10, 1909, in a fifty-foot-square enclosure. Trainers first brought in the bull and prodded him to "arouse his ire."[191] This proved to be too much, too soon because when the tiger was wheeled in in a small cage shortly thereafter, the bull was so aggressive that it injured itself trying to get into the tiger's cage and left no room for the tiger to exit to the larger cage. The tiger initially refused to exit its cage, but after prodding, it

One of many advertisements for the matchup between the bull and the tiger. *From the* El Paso Times, *January 9, 1909.*

eventually did and swiped at the bull's face. This forced the bovine to back off and allowed the tiger to enter the larger encloser.

As it emerged, the bull rushed at it, and "no sooner had the tiger emerged than the bull gored the cat's side with one of its horns." "With a screech of pain," the cat lunged at the bull and with a "terrible rush" fractured the bovine's right front leg.[192] It also began clawing at the bull's face, tearing gashes that began bleeding profusely. The animals then began stalking each other, with the bull attempting to charge, but the tiger "being able to stay out of the bull's way a good deal of the time."[193] The cat was unable to avoid the bull for long, as finally "the big maddened brute caught it."[194] The bull stepped on the tiger, "crunching its ribs," the sound of the broken bones filling the arena.[195] The bull continued to stomp on the tiger's back, while the cat lay on the ground and took bites out of the bull's legs.

Eventually, the two injured animals separated from each other, adjourned to opposite ends of the cage and refused to fight further. The degree of the injuries prompted many Americans in the audience to ask that the fight be called off, and Robert, perhaps recognizing that he might still save the expensive tiger's life, agreed, called the fight a draw and pulled all wagers. The decision and lack of action upset many members of the audience. Three Americans threw their seat cushions into the ring believing "the fight as a fake because the tiger did not put up the fight they thought he should." When the Juárez police chief asked them to leave, the men "told him to go to a warmer place than Juarez," leading the chief to temporarily detain the men.[196] When word got back to the United States of this, a number of Americans crossed the river to pressure the chief to release their countrymen, but he had already done so by the time they got there. Perhaps recognizing that the disorder would bring bad press, Robert ended the "bloody fight" by taking "up a collection for victims of a recent earthquake in Messina, Italy, collecting $125."[197]

Once again, the true fight would be held outside of the bullring, with newspaper editors allowing their political beliefs and their desire to sell papers to dictate how they reported on the event. The *San Antonio Herald* reported that the fight was horrific and that both animals had to be put down, while the *El Paso Morning Times* said it lacked action and that neither animal was seriously hurt. The *El Paso Morning Times* seems to have been more accurate, as the tiger would fight weeks later. The Humane Society–aligned *El Paso Herald* took the opportunity to jab at Porfirio Díaz's inaction in banning bullfighting by stating, "One cannot help but feel that Gen. Diaz has not accomplished all that he should have done in enlightening his people, after reading about that disgustingly brutal tiger-bull fight in Juarez Sunday."[198] The *Herald* later clarified that at least the two animals were able to fight back, unlike the horses used by picadors in the bullfights.

The response to the tiger-bull fight once again spawned a debate over animal rights in Mexico. One writer to the *Herald*, using the name "A Fellow Feeler," noted that "American sentiment holds great sway in the little sister republic and that which the big sister would condemn so decisively as to turn her back upon it would not be a popular pastime for very long."[199] The writer derided the crowd's decision to collect money for the victims of the Italian earthquake, saying that the money could be better used for animal causes. A different letter writer wrote a poem about the fights to the same effect.

As usual, the displeasure of some Americans did little to dissuade Robert, and the revenue and attention brought by the tiger-bull fight seems to have encouraged him to put on additional interspecies combat spectacles. Shortly after the fight, Robert announced a program to be held on January 24 that featured traditional bullfights as well as a wrestling match between the wrestling champion of England and the wrestling champion of Missouri. The main attraction, however, was to be four English bulldogs fighting a bull from Tayahua.

When fight day came, Robert's attendants loosed the bull in the arena. Apparently, the manager felt that the animal would make quick work of his competitors because he had had the bull's horns trimmed. This "probably saved the dogs" because soon after the animals were released into the bullring, they attacked the bull only to be "tossed on the blunt horns several times but unhurt."[200] The dogs retaliated by grabbing on to the bull's nose, neck and tongue, lacerating them but doing no critical damage. All animals survived the encounter.

Apparently, the matchup was fascinating, as one reporter described it thus: "Nothing more exciting can be imagined than these game dogs battling against a bull; every moment while they are in the ring is one of suspense, whether the bull will not toss the dogs or whether the dogs will wear the bull to the ground."[201] Little else is available on the fight except that the bulldogs "did good work."[202]

Robert followed up this event by acquiring two coyotes to fight the bulldogs in what he claimed would be a fight to the death. The sympathetic *El Paso Times* sold the event as "just one of those surprises that Manager Robert delights in springing upon the public."[203] The coyotes ended up coming from a trapper from the Triangle K Ranch in Lizard, New Mexico. Little information is available on the coyote bulldog fight, but it seems that the coyotes fared as well as could be expected against the numerically superior opponents. The bulldogs were unable to get ahold of either animal until two of the bulldogs teamed up to take down and kill the smaller of the two coyotes. The final coyote "stayed in the game" and fended off the bulldogs, making several cuts on them, but it appears that he could not overcome the overwhelming odds against him.[204]

The bulldogs were sufficiently rested that Robert put them as part of the program for the following Sunday, once again fighting a bull. The only description of the event says that "the dogs went at the bull as the latter came into the arena, and securing a fast hold, did not turn loose until the bull shook them and threw them into the air."[205] The fact that the bulldogs were not used in future fights seems to indicate they were killed in the encounter.

Although they drew crowds, these fights do not seem to have brought the numbers of the bull-buffalo battle or those involving the leopard or the tiger. Therefore, on February 9, Robert announced that he would soon host a battle royal between the now-healed Bengal tiger, a "wild Guatamape bull" and an "enormous" grizzly that had recently been captured at Jalisco.[206] The fight was to take place on February 28, 1909.

Robert took possession of the grizzly by February 13, and after the bullfights the following Sunday, he showed the animal to reporters. Newspapers said that the event promised to be "one of the most interesting sporting events seen in this section for a long time."[207] Advertisements portrayed it as a "Fight to the Death Between the Gladiators of the Wilds in the Same Cage."[208] The logistics of the event were difficult, with the *El Paso Times* making special notice of "the manner of introducing the animals and the labor necessary to get them together." A special cage had to be constructed.

Two weeks later, on February 28, 1909, the fight between the tiger, bear and bull took place at the Plaza de Toros. The *El Paso Times* called it "in some ways the best ever in that place of amusement" but offered almost no information on the event.[209] Other reporting newspapers were similarly vague. One held that the bear was gored, while another said that either the bear, the tiger or both nearly chewed off the legs of the bull. What seems most likely is that the bear was killed, the tiger severely injured and the bull emerged as the least damaged of the three.

Once again, Robert faced backlash, as did other promoters who wanted to stage their own interspecies fights. One reporter suggested "a contest between the Bengal tiger and the French master of ceremonies" or "a contest between the grizzly, the master of ceremonies and the Alcalde [mayor]" who

Robert released a bull, tiger and a bear into a cage at the same time, but because many newspapers refused to report on the animal fighting events in Juárez, little is known about the matchup. *From the* El Paso Times, *February 26, 1909.*

had allowed the events to take place.[210] Progressives in Mexico also began to place pressure on the fighting. In March 1909, female members of the SPCA of Mexico protested to the federal government when a promoter advertised that there would be a fight between a bull and a lion in the El Toreo ring. Newspapers in both the United States and Mexico printed no details about a fight between a bull, a lion and a crocodile that apparently took place at the end of March 1909 in Mexico City. The only visual from the fight was a cartoon mocking it.

The criticisms and lack of press coverage did not deter Robert from putting on a fight between a lion and a bull on July 17, 1909. Once again, there was little press coverage of the fight, which is surprising considering just how much of a disaster the fight proved to be. The few newspapers that reported on the event noted that after releasing the lion into the bull's cage, neither animal wanted to fight, refusing to move even when prodded with iron bars. The lion even appeared to go to sleep. However, when attendees finally gave up on the fight and opened the cage to retrieve the animals, the lion awoke with a start. He then "bounded to the arena, leaped the fence and gained the seats."[211] People stampeded for the exits, but they proved too small for the massive crowd, causing injuries. Others leaped over the side of the bullring, spraining ankles. Thankfully for those in attendance, there were no fatalities, as cowboys managed to lasso the lion before he could hurt anyone and dragged him back to his cage.

Indeed, after a traditional bullfight at the end of the 1909 bullfighting season, Robert announced that he would no longer put on any events in the Plaza de Toros. Instead, he traveled to California, where he announced in September 1909 that he was once again planning to tour the United States to put on "bull-teasing" exhibitions where animals would not be hurt. Robert specifically mentioned pressure from the ASPCA as one of the reasons for taking this approach. He believed that although the ASPCA would initially reject his idea, he felt that it would change its mind after it saw that he was taking measures to prevent his animals from coming to harm. Curiously, Robert seemingly relinquished any chance of gaining the APSCA's trust only a week later, when he announced that he planned to fight his Bengal tiger against a bull in Tijuana.

By this time, the tiger had seemingly grown tired of fighting bulls, so when the bout took place in Tijuana on September 19, the feline bit at the bull's nose but did little else. The bull was also in a "mutilated condition" from participating in the previous week's bullfights and saw little reason to battle.[212] After a protracted period when nothing happened, both animals were removed from the cage. After the California press eviscerated him for the Tijuana fight and his previous fights in Juárez, it seems that Robert decided to cancel his bull teasing tour and retire from the bullfighting game.

Although the Humane Society would later take credit for ending Robert's tenure as bullfighting impresario of Juárez, it is likely that the group only played a small part in the bullfighter's determination to retire. Instead, it seems that Robert decided to pursue other opportunities. Progressives had recently made gambling illegal in El Paso, leading to an exodus of Americans crossing the river to gamble in Mexico. Robert took advantage of this by opening a keno parlor in Juárez. Robert also purchased horses, which he regularly raced at the city's new horse track. Robert may have been able to afford these ventures after the May 19, 1909 death of his wealthy father-in-law, Ynocente Ochoa in Juárez. This likely led to a financial windfall for Robert and his wife.

The onset of the Mexican Revolution also likely played a role in Robert's decision to retire from bullfighting. In 1910, Juárez became home to some of the most vicious fighting of the Mexican Revolution, a ten-year-long war that resulted in more than 1 million deaths. Another 1 million residents fled to the safety of the United States. The revolution carried strong anti–United States sentiment, scaring Americans from Juárez and devastating the bullfighting and gambling business. Some Americans continued to visit the city, but they were few in number. Mexican merchants proclaimed that December 1910 was one of the worst for business.

Robert briefly emerged from retirement in 1911. With business in Juárez in decline, in March 1911, Robert planned to sell his race horses and said that he was leaving to take a job at a bullring in Marseilles, France. However, after receiving the job, he learned that the French government refused to license bullfighting in Marseilles, leading Robert to take his horses "for eastern points."[213] Instead, he somehow wound up in Salt Lake City, where he learned that Utah had lax animal cruelty laws and that progressive groups had yet to make inroads in the state. He briefly returned to El Paso to acquire bulls for a bullfighting exhibition in Utah. It is unclear how the early performances did, but Robert later purchased a buffalo from a local ranch and attempted to have it fight a matador. It seems that the buffalo-matador fight went as well as the first one, as Robert once again decided to retire after a few performances.

Robert's professional difficulties seem to have affected his marriage, as he divorced Trinidad Ochoa in 1912. In 1913, Robert traveled to France, where he married Adelaide Rebuffel. Robert believed that "the United States is the best country in the world for making money, but in France…they know how to live."[214] Apparently, Robert preferred the money because he and Adelaide moved back to El Paso and lived a well-to-do life in a $30,000 tenement house. Their romance was short-lived, as in 1916, Robert died, leaving his wife their home in El Paso. Shortly thereafter, Rebuffel married a French soldier whom she had helped recover from wounds received in World War I, but the marriage ended after the soldier tried to have her killed so he could inherit her house.

Even after Robert's retirement and subsequent death, Minnie Maddern Fiske continued to rail against bullfighting and other spectacles that harmed animals. In 1910, she wrote to the El Paso Humane Society and encouraged the organization to pass out circulars to American tourists visiting Juárez warning them about the horrors of the bullring. Fiske even sent money to cover the costs of printing. She also called for "educating the school children of Juarez against the 'sport.'" To this end, Fiske asked the El Paso Humane society to translate "The Horse's Prayer," a sympathetic portrayal of animals used by the Humane Society, into Spanish. Fiske felt that the poem, which contained the line "in the name of him who was born in a stable," would appeal to the Catholic Mexicans. In case they failed to understand the poem's message, Fiske recommended adding the line "and do not give me to the torture of the bull ring."[215] Fiske's letter also suggested buying the bullring and converting it into a baseball park.

In 1910, Fiske and members of the Humane Society funded construction of a fountain in Juárez to provide water to local animals. The hope was that it "would be a standing lesson in the objects of the Humane alliance and would be the first step in the humane work in Mexico."[216] With Fiske's encouragement, in October 1910, Benito Juárez, son of former Mexican president Benito Juárez, traveled to Washington, D.C., to attend the International Humane conference to seek the abolition of bullfighting. In June 1910, the Texas Humane Society came out with a Texas-based journal promoting animal rights called the *Texas State Humane Journal*. In 1912, Fiske passed out thousands of copies of *Black Beauty* to children in Cuba.

Fiske continued to believe that for bullfights to go away forever, Americans needed to stop attending them, so she continued her crusade. In 1921, she petitioned the U.S. Navy to ban sailors from attending bullfights when in countries where it remained legal. In 1927, she criticized Charles Lindbergh for attending bullfights in Mexico City. In 1930, while performing a play at Yale, she learned that a bloodless bullfight would be held in nearby Newark. After consulting with the local ASPCA, she called for a protest of the event.

CHAPTER 9

A STRANGE AND EPIC CONFLICT

NED THE ELEPHANT IN JUÁREZ

Ned was a fourteen-thousand-pound Siamese elephant that would one day earn a reputation for getting drunk and destroying cars. On February 2, 1913, however, he was tasked with destroying a cadre of Mexico's best fighting bulls in the Plaza de Toros before a sold-out crowd, marking the first animal-on-animal cage fight in the Juárez bullring since Felix Robert's retirement four years earlier.

Although there had been no large mammals fighting each other in the Plaza de Toros between 1909 and 1913, the bullring had not been without fighting or large mammals. On October 16, 1909, American president William Howard Taft came within eyesight of the bullring during a meeting with Mexican president Porfirio Díaz in Juárez, marking the first time a sitting American president visited Mexico. The Republican president took the opportunity to express his support for his Mexican counterpart and to announce that the two countries would both benefit from the construction of the Elephant Butte Dam in New Mexico.

After Taft's visit, the bullring continued to host bullfights, but the schedule was interrupted in November 1910 when Francisco Madero declared himself in revolution against Díaz and named himself the true president of Mexico. Madero gained the support of a team of revolutionaries who disagreed with Díaz, resented foreign interference in Mexico and wanted substantial social and economic reform. In the north, this included Pascual Orozco, Francisco "Pancho" Villa and Giuseppi Garibaldi II. The revolutionaries gathered their supporters and rallied to Madero's call, managing to capture most of Chihuahua from Díaz's federal forces by February 1911.

That month, Federalist general and Díaz ally Juan G. Navarro occupied Juárez, sequestered the bullring to station his horses there and dug trenches around the city to defend it against rebel attack. With Navarro entrenched, Madero felt that it would be a waste of resources to capture Juárez, and so he ordered Villa, Orozco and Garibaldi to fall back. They did not listen. On May 8, 1911, they moved on Juárez, and at midnight, a group of American mercenaries allied with the insurgents captured the bullring. The rest of the city fell to the rebels shortly thereafter. The capture of Juárez proved decisive to the overall revolution, and Díaz resigned on May 25, 1911, allowing Madero to assume the presidency.

Madero was a vegetarian who had received support from the Animal Protection Association of Mexico and other progressive groups in the early days of his revolution. Therefore, among his first acts after assuming power, the new president banned bullfighting, horse racing and gambling in Mexico. The rulings did not stick. The revolutionaries who had fought to take Juárez did not share Madero's convictions, so they ignored the president's orders and instead put on bullfights to pay their troops. Slaughtered bulls fed the revolutionary army. Because Madero had to face multiple rebellions from opponents on the left and right, he could not afford to upset his allies by enforcing the ban, especially considering that Juárez was so distant from his capital in Mexico City.

The lack of attention from the federal government meant that for the next year and a half, Juárez would have fewer rules than it had under Díaz. Not only did the bullfights continue in spite of Madero's ban, but Juárez even hosted a boxing match, something expressly prohibited in Mexico since Billy Clarke fought Billy Smith in Hidalgo. The fight was between Kid Mitchell and Jack Herrick. The two had originally planned to hold their bout in New Mexico, which had just become a state and was therefore no longer under federal restrictions banning boxing in the territories. Unfortunately for the two men, the newly created state government also banned prizefighting, prompting the decision to hold the bout across the border. On May 19, 1912, Mitchell and Herrick fought twenty rounds in the Juárez bullring in front of four thousand fans, many of whom were American.

Promoters and revolutionaries looking to profit took notice of the attendance because few Americans had been crossing into Juárez since 1910. The constant fighting had made the city too dangerous for American tastes, especially considering that some revolutionaries carried strong anti-American sentiment. The tenuous legal status of bullfights and gambling in Juárez also deterred tourism. However, the Mitchell and Herrick bout showed that Americans would come back for novelty, and according to one story, this prompted a group of entrepreneurs in Juárez to travel to the United States in the hopes of not only reviving the interspecies fighting that had happened under Robert but also outdoing it by bringing the biggest mammal in the western hemisphere to fight in Juárez.

Little is known about Ned's early years, but at a young age, Siamese workers captured him and put him to work stacking lumber. Ned had little trouble carrying out this task considering his strong, well-muscled trunk and massive size. Even as a young bull he had enormous forehead domes that "looked like battering rams" and long tusks that would eventually grow to be seven feet long.

In about 1902, Americans looking for elephants to sell to circuses in the United States purchased Ned and sold him to the Great Syndicate Shows of Missouri. Trainers at that circus found the young elephant too cantankerous to teach; he had little tolerance for instruction and reacted violently whenever his trainers tried to make him do anything he did not want to do. Within a year, the Great Syndicate Shows sold Ned to the Great Eastern Shows, which likewise found the animal too difficult to manage, so it turned around and sold Ned to the Clark Circus in 1903.

At the time, the Clark Circus was a small operation run by Mack Loren Clark. The circus had only one other elephant, a two-humped camel that had once had its throat slit by a drunk Texan, a few ponies for children to ride and a rotating group of clowns and acrobats. However, Clark aspired to be a major circus, and he believed that the gargantuan Ned would make a great centerpiece. He coupled the purchase with a series of good business decisions and hired quality employees to help him run his company. His management team included his two sons, who helped him with the day-to-day operations of the circus.

The man who trained Ned in the Clark Circus was Aboriginal Australian William Badger, also known as Bill Badger, "Old Badger" or "Midnight Badger." The latter nickname was a reference to his dark skin, with newspapers of the time describing him as "black as Cyclops from the forge."[217] Badger began his career as a cook for the Sells Brothers' Circus when it toured Australia in the mid-1800s. When the tour ended, Sells Brothers' management let Badger and other temporary employees go and packed their animals and permanent staff on board a ship to return to the United States.

Fascinated with circus life, Badger stowed away and took up in the elephant's storage room. When food later went missing and the ship's crew

125

tried to search the elephant's room for stowaways, they were unable to do so because the animals acted as if they were angry and showed signs of attacking anyone who entered. It would later be learned that Badger was poking the large mammals with a stick to rile them up to scare away the searchers. Weeks in the hold with the elephants taught Badger how to get the animals to do what he wanted. Thanks to his skills, Sells Brothers' hired him as a permanent trainer when the ship finished its Pacific voyage.

When he first became a trainer, Badger treated elephants with kindness, but by the time he became Ned's trainer, he had come to regard the animals as "the trickiest beasts that live." Sounding like a spurned paramour, Badger said of elephants, "They'll fool you for a long time by allowing you to think they love you, when they are just waiting for the chance to put you out of business with a swing of the snaky snout of theirs."[218] Badger's opinions were not without evidence, as one of the elephants he cared for had killed four trainers, and Badger would see at least a dozen trainers killed by elephants over his career.

By the time Badger came to care for Ned, he had adopted the viewpoint that "I hate them, though I am trainer. I rule them by brutality and fear, not by kindness."[219] Although cruel, Badger's methods appear to have been successful, at least for circuses, and he remained regularly employed. After leaving the Sells circus and a tenure tending elephants for P.T. Barnum, Badger joined the Clark Circus to care for its growing stable of elephants. The trainer would ride alongside the elephants atop his spotted horse, "Robert," making sure that the animals stayed in line when traveling between towns.

Using his firm methodology, Badger and the Clarks taught Ned a variety of tricks. Ned could stand on a tub and turn around, raise himself on his front two feet or his two hind feet, sit down, lie down and even waltz. Clark would later claim that Ned was the first elephant to do a head stand. More impressively, Ned could walk on bottles or two-foot-high pegs the diameter of a soda can. However, as Ned grew, the pegs and bottles could no longer support his weight. Clark was not disappointed by this development because once fully grown, Ned was larger than Jumbo, the previous record holder for largest elephant in North America. Indeed, by 1910, Ned was the largest land animal in the Western Hemisphere.

This size meant that whenever the pachyderm came to town, crowds flocked to see him, growing the circus's profits and allowing Clark to invest in additional animals and attractions. By 1910, the circus could claim eighteen cages of wild creatures, including 210 horses, 8 camels and 4 elephants.

Promoters billed Ned as the largest elephant in the world. Although the Clarks took credit for training Ned, his future keeper George Lewis believed that "the old man [Badger] was the only one Ned would allow to give him orders." *From the* Al G. Barnes Circus Route Book, *1923.*

Clark also purchased his own train cars, which he used to ferry the circus from one town in the United States to the next.

Ned not only drew crowds but also helped the circus in other ways. He was so powerful that he could pull tent stakes out of the ground after performances, and Badger also taught him to be a "Hey Rube" elephant. As illustrated in the *Adventures of Huckleberry Finn,* circuses in the late nineteenth and early twentieth centuries could be raucous, as they were one of only a few social events in many rural communities. Crowds used such occasions to get drunk and talk politics, a combination that often led to violence. Audiences also often got rowdy when they suspected that circus personnel were ripping them off, and they occasionally attacked circus members and destroyed equipment. When this happened, employees would yell "Hey Rube!" to rally the other members of the circus to their defense. Apparently, Badger realized that the best way to disperse a crowd and restore order was with an elephant because he taught Ned to hold a tent stake and swing it at crowds on command.

Although useful and profitable, Ned was not happy under Badger's oppressive thumb, and he would take any chance he could to get back at his trainers. Although he never seriously harmed anyone, Ned threw trainers regularly and tormented them in other ways when possible. Once in Louisiana, a trainer hoped to escape an angry Ned by taking refuge in a blacksmith shop, but the elephant broke down one of the building's walls. Ned also took every opportunity to escape. One day, while the circus was traveling through Pennsylvania, Ned broke out of his bonds and ran into the countryside. Trainers found him dancing on nearby patch of asphalt.

There are different stories about how Ned's fight with the bulls of Juárez in 1913 came to be. In the simplest one, promoters from the Juárez bullring learned about the massive elephant. Hoping to lure American crowds back to Juárez during a lull in revolutionary violence, they traveled to the United States and sought out Clark, asking if they could pit his animal against bulls. Clark accepted the offer.

The other explanation holds that the fight came together out of happenstance. In 1913, the Clark Circus arrived in El Paso, and Clark, as he often did when arriving in a new city, sought permission to hold a parade promoting his show. Although the city council had passed the law banning parades advertising bullfights, circuses did not fall under the legislation because no harm came to the animals. Clark had no trouble receiving a permit and marched his animals and performers down San Antonio Street in El Paso. With a brass band preceding him, Ned marched along, bearing a placard proclaiming that he was the "World's Mightiest Pachyderm."[220] Apparently some Mexicans in the crowd took offense to the "mighty" claim and began taunting Ned and his owner, claiming that Ned could not stand up to a fighting bull. Clark fired back, "Shucks you don't know what a good elephant can do," and an argument ensued.[221] In this second version of events, it was only after hearing about the argument that the management of the Juárez bullring traveled to El Paso to speak with Clark about pitting Ned against some of its bulls.

Whichever version is correct, the promoters offered Clark $3,000 to fight Ned against five bulls, although sources are unclear if they expected him to fight all the animals at the same time. Perhaps of greater value, they also told the circus owner that they planned to make a motion picture recording of the event and that Clark would receive a copy of the film. He would also keep a share of the film rights, which promoters intended to sell to Thomas Edison's motion picture company for display in theaters throughout the United States.

Since the start of the Mexican Revolution, numerous Hollywood camera crews had descended on the border to capture footage of the war, so producers in California would then craft a story around the footage. The movies included *The Greaser's Gauntlet*, *Sin and the Greasers* and *The Greaser*, and as could be expected with these titles, the plots of the movies often involved an Anglo battling treacherous Mexicans. Two motion pictures, *Handicap* and *A Mexican Courtship*, had even been filmed in the Juárez bullring in 1912. (The latter movie is in the public domain and can be viewed on YouTube. It contains graphic scenes of actual bullfights in the Plaza de Toros.)

Possibly imagining what a movie about his elephant would mean for his circus, Clark agreed to these terms, and he and the Juárez managers set the event for 3:45 p.m. on Sunday, February 2, 1913. The *El Paso Times* ran advertisements throughout January, with teases that the "Monster Elephant 'Ned' will be pitted in the ring against the most ferocious bulls that ever entered the Juarez Bull Ring in a fight to the death."[222] Box seat tickets went for $1.50, shaded seats $1.25 and seats in the sun $1.00. Children under eight got in for half price. The *El Paso Herald*, as it had done for all interspecies fights and bullfights since 1907, refused to promote the event.

Clark was able to secure a permit to hold a second parade advertising the fight across the border in spite of El Paso's ban on advertising bullfights and displays of animal cruelty. The chief of police would later claim that he did not know about the bans on parades promoting animal cruelty, but it is also possible that he thought he was granting permission for Clark to hold another parade to promote his circus. Local animal rights activists suspected that the chief was on the take or that he chose not to enforce the law because he did not believe in it. Whatever the case, the chief ignored their protests and refused to rescind the permit.

The second parade took place on February 1, the day before the fight. Clark and the Mexican promoters obviously saw the chance to stir up controversy

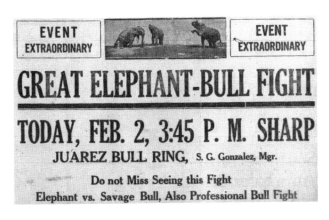

EVENT EXTRAORDINARY **EVENT EXTRAORDINARY**

GREAT ELEPHANT-BULL FIGHT

TODAY, FEB. 2, 3:45 P. M. SHARP

JUÁREZ BULL RING, S. G. Gonzalez, Mgr.

Do not Miss Seeing this Fight

Elephant vs. Savage Bull, Also Professional Bull Fight

Advertisement for the elephant-bull fight to take place in Juárez. *From* El Paso Morning Times, *February 2, 1913.*

because the second parade was led by a band made up of Mexican federal soldiers playing "Invincible Eagle," a 1901 song by American John Philip Sousa meant to show patriotism toward the United States. The march concluded with Ned, wrapped up in a canvas proclaiming, "This African elephant will fight a ferocious bull from Chicucha [*sic*] to the death in the bull ring in Juarez tomorrow." The sign carried the prices for tickets.[223]

With news of the fight spreading, church officials attempted to shame their parishioners into staying away from Juárez. Reverend R.T. Hanks noted that "with the Mexican end of the affair, we have nothing to do, for there is no possible way by which we can influence the powers that be over there to do the decent thing." However, he called on El Pasoans to "exert our influence to keep people from patronizing so brutal and disgraceful a performance," citing a story about a man turning down an invitation from a woman to attend a bullfight because he was a "gentleman." Either repeating himself or trying to make a point, Reverend Hanks said, "The other thing we can do in this matter is to use our influence to keep people from patronizing that inhuman, brutal affair."[224] He then called on his flock to vote out men like the police chief who overlooked animal rights violations.

Unfortunately for the progressive preacher, the shaming was ineffective, as the event sold some five thousand tickets and would be held as planned. The day of the fight, Badger, Clark and Clark's son, Lee, put a chain on Ned and walked him across the international bridge into Juárez. It seems that Clark had some last-minute reservations and worried that Ned was not up to the task, but Badger, having witnessed Ned's brutality on multiple occasions, reassured him that the elephant could take care of himself. The men arrived to find the bullring "jammed with cheering gringos and jeering Mexicans."[225] Apparently, there were so many people that "there was not room enough in the arena for another person and many were standing in the doorway."[226]

Shortly before the fight, Badger or Lee Clark tied a red sash to Ned's neck and one to his tail to serve as flags to agitate the bulls into attacking. When fight time came, Badger attached a twenty-foot chain to Ned, marched him to the center of the ring and nailed a spike into the ground, to which he attached Ned's chain. No one wanted the elephant to escape and harm a spectator. Once this was done, Badger signaled for a bugle to be sounded, indicating that the fight should start.

Although one version of events has multiple bulls being loosed at once to face Ned, most versions of the story indicate that Ned first faced off against a single bull. An attendee lifted a gate allowing the animal to enter the bullring, and as it passed through the opening, another attendee sitting

Ned preparing to take on a bull. The image shows a flag tied around Ned's neck to encourage the bull to attack. *Getty Research Institute.*

on the fence stuck a banderillo into his back to anger him. Little is known about the bull except that he was "a good-sized animal with rather short and sharp horns."[227]

As one version of the story goes, when the bull was unleashed in the ring, Ned grew scared and stretched his chain as far away from the strange animal as he could go. It seems that the bull took the elephant's fear as weakness and charged him. Ned, apparently moving away from the bull, did not see him coming, allowing the bull to hit him full bore in his flank, sending the elephant toppling to its side. Such an outcome seems improbable, especially considering that Ned weighed some fourteen thousand pounds and the bull was almost certainly less than two thousand, but it is physically possible. Indeed, a two-thousand-pound bull traveling some thirty miles per hour could impart eighty-eight thousand pounds of force on an object, easily enough to topple a seven-ton elephant. A photograph of the event seems to confirm that Ned went down, as it depicts the elephant on his haunches.

However, there is another possible explanation for the photograph. One account of the fight has the bull charging Ned, but when he nears, the elephant, having been taught to balance on his hind legs and do handstands,

stands up and either kicks his opponent with one of his front feet or tries to stomp the bull. Whatever the case, it seems that when the momentum-driven bull met the elephant's foot, it floored the charging animal. At that point, Ned then tried to roll over on his attacker, and it is this scenario that is depicted in the photograph.

Whether it was a kick to the face, an elephant rolling over on him or some unrecorded attack by Ned, the bull soon determined that he wanted nothing to do with his much larger opponent. After only a few minutes in the ring, he ran as far away from Ned as he could and refused to fight any longer. This prompted the crowd to boo and demand the bull be taken out.

Artist depiction of the bull rushing Ned. *From the* Tensas Gazette, *June 20, 1913.*

The organizers complied, unleashing a second bull into the ring instead. Just like his predecessor, the new combatant seemed game and began circling around his larger opponent. Unfortunately for him, Ned was now prepared, and when the bull charged him, the elephant successfully "parried a thrust with his tusks."[228] When the bull came near a second time, the elephant used his trunk, which weighed some four hundred pounds and was home to some forty thousand muscles, to send his opponent "heading in the other direction."[229] Another person said that Ned "with his trunk laid out his antagonists whenever he could reach them."[230] It seems that the trunk, strengthened through years of carrying logs in Siam, left the second bull "all bruised up" and so hurt that it tried to jump over the fence to escape his large foe.[231]

It was around this time that the promoters unleashed three additional bulls, but they, smartly, refused to engage the large pachyderm. This prompted staff matadors to come out and wave their flags between the bulls and Ned to trick the bulls into charging the elephant. When this did not meet the proper response, banderilleros attached firecrackers to the end of their pikes and stuck them in the bulls, hoping that the explosions would put the animals in a fury. What happened next varies wildly across sources. In one account, even goaded by firecrackers, the bulls refused to engage. In another, the prodding worked, and one of the animals charged and "slightly pricked" Ned before realizing what he had done. Infuriated again, Ned supposedly picked up the animal with his trunk and "deliberately threw" it from the bullring.[232]

At this point, it seems that either Ned escaped his bonds or the scene in the bullring became so chaotic that the other two bulls and the matadors came within the range of the elephant's trunk because Ned was able to grab the other two animals in succession and toss them as well. He "then made a complete cleanup by tossing several matadors and attendants far up in the bleachers and then seized a matador's cloak with his trunk, waved it around and threw it upon his head, all to the delight of the Americans in the audience."[233] A different account of the story has Ned goring one of the bulls with his tusk and parading it around the ring as a trophy.

Apparently, the Mexicans in the audience either took offense to the way Ned had treated the bulls and matadors, or, as another version of the story says, they were upset that Ned had not killed all the bulls, as had been advertised and as they had come to expect from such fights. Whatever version is true, a huge brawl erupted in the stands. In one version of the story, members of the crowd spilled into the bullring seeking vengeance on Ned for besting their bulls, forcing the elephant and his trainers to take refuge in a paddock.

In a more plausible version of events, Mexican police attempted to placate the raucous crowd by placing Ned in custody in one of the bullring's stalls and informed Clark that he could retrieve his animal only after paying a $500 fine. The charge was either failing to deliver the program advertised or for causing a public disturbance. The police also confiscated the film reels of the event. Still a different version of the story holds that the promoters, either upset at the fight's outcome or the chaos that had followed, were the ones to lock up Ned, and they were the ones to demand $500 for lost revenue and to cover the cost of what Ned had eaten while in Juárez. In all versions of the story, the promoters refused to pay Clark the $3,000 promised for the fight.

Whatever version of events is more accurate, it seems that Clark and company knew that they could do nothing about the film reels or the lost $3,000, but they refused to leave Ned in Mexico until local courts could decide his fate. They were almost certainly aware that a judicial review might take days, weeks or even longer and that a trial in Juárez was likely to favor the bullring promoters, not some Americans and their Australian employee. Therefore, the Clarks and Badger decided to break Ned out.

Lee Clark and Badger snuck into the bullring and approached the holding pen in which Ned was being kept, but they discovered that the gate had been locked. Recognizing that the wooden enclosure could not contain the full force of a fourteen-thousand-pound animal, Badger ordered Ned to "come out of there."[234] Ned did as commanded, smashing through the gate and ripping it off its hinges. With a portion of the wooden barrier still hanging from Ned's neck, the trio made their way in the direction of the nearby international bridge.

Apparently, someone heard the noise of the breakout because a crowd formed and tried to prevent the elephant and circus men from escaping to the United States. Ned responded by lifting Badger with his trunk and placing him on his head. Badger quickly came up with a plan. He or Lee Clark handed Ned a wooden stake, which the elephant took in his trunk. Having been a "Hey Rube" elephant, Ned had been "trained to swing it back and forth in front of him."[235] When would-be attackers came to attack him or members of the circus, the great beast slashed at them with its stake, clearing a path to the bridge and El Paso.

Before they could reach the bridge, a car turned in front of Ned, attempting to block his progress. Ned responded by bowling over the car and continued his escape. Although this detail sounds implausible, it would not be the only time Ned would make short work of a motor vehicle that got in his way. The group made it back to El Paso, where they relayed what happened to the rest of the circus.

Compared to previous interspecies fights, newspapers carried little news of the event. Those that did had few details on the actual combat and almost nothing on what transpired after the fight. The *El Paso Times*, which frequently carried detailed accounts of animal fights during Felix Robert's time and still took advertising dollars from bullfight promoters, lauded the novelty of the battle and dedicated multiple paragraphs to describing the fight. The *Times*, however, provided no background explaining how the fight came together and nothing on its aftermath.

Other Texas papers made light of the spectacle or criticized it. A columnist in the *Amarillo Daily News* used it to make a political commentary about the recent 1912 presidential election in the United States, which had featured Bull Moose Party candidate Teddy Roosevelt facing off against Republican William Howard Taft. This led one columnist to remark, "Battles between a bull and elephant in the Juarez arena, shows that American political methods have crossed the border."[236] As expected, the *El Paso Herald* carried few details about the event. Instead, it once again served as a mouthpiece for animal rights groups. They blamed the El Paso chief of police, indecent Mexicans and godless Americans for the success of the fight and warned that by allowing such displays to take place, they were inviting mob rule.

The lack of attention from the press may have owed to animal rights activists pressuring newspapers to not report on the event or to a general decrease in sensationalistic journalism. Beginning in the aftermath of the Spanish-American War, which some blamed on New York newspapers' false and exaggerated claims, many journalists called for ethical reporting. This included a decrease in sensationalism and an appeal for reporters to focus on events that were more important to civilized society. In some regards, this could be seen as a progressive reform meant to curb what the average citizen was exposed to. The lack of coverage may also have been for a less noble reason: a different elephant fight won headlines. The day after Ned's fight, a lion in a Connecticut zoo escaped its enclosure and attacked a camel, but an elephant came to the rescue. The pachyderm lifted the lion up and smashed him to the ground. When the lion tried to leap at the elephant's head, it "was knocked senseless by one blow from the trunk of the maddened pachyderm."[237]

The men of the Clark Circus never saw the $3,000 the promoters had promised them, nor did they receive the film footage of the event, which remains lost to this day. At least they left Mexico with a story. Lee Clark would later remember the event as "the major circus comedy drama. It is full of pathos, comedy, and heroic action."[238] Unfortunately, Badger and the elder Clark would not live long to tell the tale. Badger died shortly after the fight around 1915. M.L. Clark progressively handed over control of the circus to his sons before he died in 1926.

Ned survived them both, but he would live an occasionally calamitous and at other times pitiful life for his remaining years. In 1921, the Clarks apparently determined that without Badger to keep Ned in line, the elephant was not worth the trouble, and so they sold the animal to Al G. Barnes Stonehouse, who ran the Al G. Barnes Big 4 Ring Wild Animal Circus. Stonehouse gave Ned the new name Tusko and called him the "Mighty Monarch of the Jungle."[239]

Ned's new owners also found the elephant difficult to control. In 1922, less than a year after buying the elephant, the Al G. Barnes Circus made a stop in Sedro-Woolley, Washington, where Ned threw one of his keepers thirty feet in the air and made a run for it. For the rest of the day, Ned made his way through Sedro-Woolley, knocking over telephone poles, garages, fences and chicken coops as he made his escape. He crushed a Model T under his hoofs and used his trunk to overturn other cars. Although destructive, Ned's rampage did not appear dangerous to humans, and the people of the town stayed out of Ned's way and enjoyed the show.

That was until Ned caught a whiff of sour mash emanating from the local tavern. Likely to avoid new prohibition laws, the tavern was cooking its own booze. Ned smashed into the tavern and "gorged on the sour mash," quickly growing drunk.[240] He then apparently decided that a nearby house had wronged him. He went over to it, peered through the windows and, after frightening the inhabitants, proceeded to knock the home off its foundation. He then broke into the nearby barn and feasted on the hay stored there before running off to continue his rampage.

For the rest of the night, Ned ran through the darkness, getting into fights with automobiles and houses, damaging some twenty cars and knocking down the walls of three homes. By morning the following day, he had traveled some thirty miles to the town of Garden of Eden, where the men of the circus finally caught up to him strolling on a side road. In total, he had caused some $20,000 in property damage, which Stonehouse had to pay out to the people of Sedro-Woolley. Fortunately, the only person harmed in the rampage was Ned's trainer, who suffered bruised ribs.

The press relished telling the story about the destructive but seemingly harmless elephant, allowing Stonehouse to capitalize on Ned's new notoriety. Unfortunately, the elephant's behavior grew progressively more violent over the ensuing years, and he more frequently attacked, although never killed, his trainers. This led Stonehouse to begin shackling Ned's legs and tying his tusks down so he could not lift his head. The circus even developed a chain

Tusko got loose and ran wild for two days.

World's *Meanest* Elephant

After his fight in Mexico, Ned drew newspaper headlines after he destroyed part of a town and faced down the National Guard. *From the* Atlanta Journal, *April 19, 1931.*

136

straight jacket to completely immobilize Ned, and he sometimes remained locked up for months on end. Perhaps owing to this unusual garb, his atrophied muscles or the fact that he now went by Tusko, in 1929, when the Al G. Barnes Circus arrived in El Paso, no one seemed to recognize that this was the same elephant that had fought bulls in Juárez sixteen years before.

Later that year, Ned had to watch as members of the circus used submachine guns to execute fellow elephant Black Diamond in Corsicana, Texas, after that animal threw its trainer over a car and impaled a woman with its tusk, killing her. Black Diamond's deed and Ned's progressively aggressive behavior convinced Stonehouse that he no longer wanted to use male elephants in his show. They were too unruly. Therefore, in 1931, he sold Ned to a carnival barker, who kept the elephant chained to a wall as a side show. Apparently, Ned liked this life even less than being in the circus because in 1931, he ripped his bonds from the wall and went on a rampage, ripping down multiple buildings before being caught.

Not long after, Ned was sold to new owners, who brought him to Portland, where he was once again shackled, tied to a concrete pillar and put on display. Once again, Ned determined that he did not want to be shackled. On Christmas Day 1931, the elephant pulled the pin from the shackles holding his front feet and began straining to break free from the chain tying his back feet to the concrete pillar. His owners could not get close enough to reshackle Ned, so they had to watch as the elephant stretched himself as far as possible and broke everything he could get his front feet and trunk on, including a steel-reinforced concrete wall. Fearing that the elephant would eventually break out, the mayor of Portland called in the National Guard, who trained their weapons on the animal. Fortunately, Ned's owners were able to fashion a snare to reshackle the elephant's front feet.

The standoff with the National Guard made Ned a popular figure in the Pacific Northwest, and his owners capitalized on the popularity by leasing the elephant for advertising. He appeared at baseball games and fairs, demolished houses as part of an ad campaign for a house-wrecking company and marched in parades. Ned's owners never acquired the proper licenses to exhibit the animal, leading the district attorney of Seattle to seize the elephant and place him in the Woodland Park Zoo until his owners could pay the city what they owed. While in the zoo, Ned became a popular attraction, but he continued to resist captivity, throwing trainers, tubs and everything else within reach of his trunk.

Unfortunately, Ned would not live long in the zoo. In 1933, he suffered an embolism and died. (It should be noted that Ned was not the same elephant named Tusko that died after scientists administered him a massive dosage of LSD. That Tusko passed in Oklahoma in 1962.) Although the elephant's owners wanted to have his body stuffed for continued use as a side show, this does not appear to have happened. His bones somehow ended up in the biology department at the University of Oregon, where students studied them well into the 1950s.

Newspapers carried stories about Ned's life and accounts from those who knew him. Some of the articles were negative, with one saying, "A drunk is a drunk wherever you find him, and that big elephant was no exception."[241] A trainer eulogized him by saying, "He had the psychological attitude of a juvenile delinquent or a man who has served time in the penitentiary."[242] People expected the worst of him, and he knew it.

Most accounts, however, were positive, reflecting favorably on the elephant's life and framing his bad behavior as nothing more than mischief. They noted that although Ned caused extensive property damage, he never killed anyone. Some saw his aggressiveness as understandable, considering how he had been treated by his various owners. Others said that his destructive tendencies were a reaction to his time in Mexico. One newspaper went so far as to claim that Ned spent his last years "dreaming of the gay, glad days when he tossed all those bulls, matadors and picadors into the grandstand at Juarez."[243]

The *New York Daily News* carried a poem eulogy to the fallen elephant written by Ed Sullivan:

> *Giants in strength these elephants are,*
> *Stronger than any man or beast ever to tenant the Garden.*
> *There was Tusko, Al G. Barnes' Goliath!*
> *At Juarez, Mexico.*
> *The bull-ring owners, their business hurt by the circus,*
> *Scoffed at the elephant, and offered to pit*
> *Their fighting bulls against him.*
> *So Tusko went into the bull-ring, his beady eyes eager.*
> *He kicked the first bull to death, and*
> *Three more bulls charged into the arena.*
> *Tusko hurled them, one by one, into the arena seats,*
> *It was a strange and epic conflict, but at its close,*
> *Tusko trumpeted in victory!*[244]

CONCLUSION

I n 1914, Minnie Maddern Fiske reported that she was "greatly pleased when informed that the bull fights were not so frequent in Juárez as of old."[245] It was not just bullfighting, as there had not been another interspecies fight since Ned the elephant's battle the previous year, and although Fiske would not have known it at the time, more than a decade and a half would pass before the border hosted another fight between large mammals when a lion once again faced off against a bull in Juárez. After that, the next widely reported matchup was a Bengal tiger against a bull in Reynosa in 1958.

What happened? Why were there more than a dozen staged interspecies fights involving large mammals from 1895 to 1913, but so few after?

There is little question that the violence of the Mexican Revolution was the main factor in bringing the interspecies fights to end. One week after Ned took on the bulls in the Plaza de Toros, General Victoriano Huerta overthrew and soon thereafter assassinated Mexican president Francisco Madero. The revolutionaries who had helped Madero rise to power reorganized their armies and marched on Huerta, descending Mexico further into chaos. Pancho Villa seized control of the north and continued to fight federal authorities even after Huerta resigned and Villa's former ally Venustiano Carranza took over the government of Mexico.

Revolutionaries and federal soldiers knew that proximity to the United States meant access to guns and other supplies, so cities on the Mexican side of the border became battlegrounds. One army or another turned bullrings to rubble, Spanish bullfighters fled to Europe and Americans refused to cross the river to attend events out of fear of catching a stray bullet. The border became even more dangerous after Pancho Villa raided New Mexico in 1916, and the United States responded by sending soldiers into Mexico to catch him, inflaming an already tense situation. Newspapers that once encouraged Americans to visit their southern neighbors now warned them to stay away. With an abundance of violence and no Americans to whom to cater, promoters saw little reason to put on the unusual spectacles that had been a staple of the border for the previous decades.

The situation led Fiske to comment that she "deplored the warfare that is now tearing Mexico, but thought it had at least contributed to one good cause in temporarily stopping the bull fights in many localities."[246] Indeed, the war had accomplished what Fiske, the Humane Society and the ASPCA had failed to achieve using political means. The City of El Paso's bans on parades and pamphlets promoting bullfights had temporarily hurt attendance at Robert's shows, but in a way, they only encouraged the promoter to stage more bizarre stunts to lure audiences. In 1917, the Humane Society helped fund Venustiano Carranza's campaign for president, and after he won, he banned bullfighting. Distant from Mexico City and with the revolution still raging, the mayor of Juárez, Melchor Herrera, not only ignored the president's decree, but soon after receiving word of the pronouncement, Herrera also held his own bullfight in the Plaza de Toros, roping and riding a bull to the delight of eight thousand in attendance. As historian David Dorado Romo noted, in this instance, "The spectacle had proven mightier than the revolution."[247]

Animal rights groups' efforts to stop the fights using social and economic pressure had likewise met with mixed results. Having Mark Twain write an anti-bullfighting story and handing out copies of *Black Beauty* may have had a long-term impact on the perception of the various fights involving animals, but there is little to indicate that it hurt ticket sales in the short term. The progressive crusade to discourage newspapers from reporting on the events seems to have been at least somewhat effective, as detailed accounts of fights became rarer after 1908, but this might have owed more to an end to "yellow journalism" than to their campaign.

Indeed, the Joseph Pulitzer–owned *St. Louis Post Dispatch* and William Randolph Hearst's *San Francisco Examiner* were the most popular and most sensational newspapers in the western United States at the turn of the twentieth century, and in a bid to lure readers, the two papers often provided more details on the border fights than even local news outlets. By the 1910s, however, both newspapers had adopted a more measured approach to journalism after receiving criticism for their sensational reporting. They eschewed the niche and macabre that had been the foundations of their brands and focused more on public interest stories. Newspapers throughout the United States followed their lead, and stories about the exotic fights in Mexico grew even more rare, further hurting potential ticket sales.

The fights also came to an end because Americans and Mexicans found other outlets for entertainment. Baseball grew in popularity on both sides of the border in the early twentieth century, and boxing returned south of it. Mexican politicians after Porfirio Díaz did not share their predecessor's distaste for prizefighting, and the nation eventually lifted its ban on the sport. After the 1912 bout between Kid Mitchell and Jack Herrick in Juárez, legal boxing matches became regular occurrences on the border, meaning Americans did not have to settle for alternatives to their favorite fight sport. Over time, Mexicans also grew to enjoy boxing, and before long, they preferred it to bullfighting or forms of combat involving animals.

The spread of cinema also certainly played a role in bringing the border animal spectacles to an end. Between 1910 and 1920, more than a dozen movie houses opened in El Paso. The movies featured in these theaters depicted exotic locales, people and animals in stories featuring romance, mystery and, of course, violence. Promoters no longer needed to physically bring animals and violence to the border when filmgoers could just watch these things on a screen. Cinema also drove many circuses and vaudeville acts out of business, indirectly limiting the pool of animal fighters. Owing to traveling circuses, the Texas-Mexico border in the late 1800s and early 1900s had been home to more exotic large mammals than any time since the Pleistocene, when most new-world megafauna went extinct, and around half of the large mammal combatants in the border fights had once been part of a vaudeville show. The only circuses to survive the expansion of cinema were larger and more reputable ones that would be less likely to tarnish their reputation by pitting one of their animals against another in a fight.

The Mexican Revolution, the efforts of progressive groups, the reduction in sensational journalism and the emergence of alternative forms of entertainment meant that there were few fights involving large exotic species after 1913, but some forms of animal combat continued into the twentieth century. North of the border, bulldogging is still an event in many rodeos, although animal rights groups, including the ASPCA, are fighting to bring the sport to an end. Bullfighting remains popular in parts of Mexico, but many states have outlawed the practice. Both the United States and the

Mexican sides of the border are also still home to illegal animal fights. Law enforcement in both nations frequently uncover underground cockfighting and dogfighting matches despite federal and state laws banning the events. Mexican promoters also still hold events wherein they tape a knife to the right hands of two monkeys, bind their left hands together and allow frustration to descend into violence for the viewing pleasure of American tourists.

Although animal fights continue to occur, they are not well known in the United States or Mexico, and they receive little press attention—the fights are certainly not the subject of full-page newspaper articles as the lion versus bull battles were in the early 1900s. Even bulldogging and bullfighting, while still legal in some areas, are niche sports with little appeal to the general public. There are also no fights on the economic scale of what happened from 1895 to 1913. No one is willing to defy the law and spend tens of thousands of dollars for a tiger or elephant only to see the animals die in their first fight or have the law seize the animals before an event can even take place.

For these reasons, the time from 1895 to 1913 on the Texas-Mexico border remains exceptional, with only ancient Rome being comparable in the brutality and peculiarity of its staged animal fights. Like Rome, the United States was a regional power with a large population and expendable capital. Like the Romans, a portion of the American people wanted to spend their capital on blood sport, and opportunistic individuals—government officials in Rome, promoters on the border—sought to appease the masses with gladiatorial fights involving animals. Transportation improvements and the expansion of vaudeville meant that the people of the United States had access to large mammals just as the Romans did, and whereas the Romans had little compunction glorifying their games, for a time, many Americans felt the same about the events on the border. Owing to changing laws and attitudes toward animals, it is unlikely that similar conditions will emerge any time soon, meaning ancient Rome and the Texas-Mexico border at the dawn of the twentieth century will remain exceptional in the scale, cruelty and outrageousness of their spectacles.

NOTES

Introduction

1. *El Paso Times*, "Juarez Bull Ring," February 26, 1909.
2. Schell, "Lions, Bulls, and Baseball," 266.
3. *El Paso Times*, "Sunday's Fight."
4. Ibid.

Chapter 1

5. *Philadelphia Inquirer*, "Forepaugh's Shows."
6. *Idaho Statesman*, "Down in San Francisco."
7. *Los Angeles Herald*, "Parnell and the Bear."
8. *Los Angeles Herald*, "Lion and Bear."
9. *Morning Call*, "Lion and Bear Fight."
10. *Denver Post*, "Lion and the Grizzly."
11. Ibid.
12. *Illinois State Register*, "Grizzly Bested Lion."

Chapter 2

13. *The Inquirer*, "Animal Combat."

14. Ibid.
15. *Times-Democrat*, "Lion Tamer's Arm Badly Mangled."
16. *Inter Ocean*, "Victim of a Vicious Lion."
17. *San Francisco Examiner*, "Battle to the Death."
18. *The Inquirer*, "Animal Combat."
19. *San Francisco Examiner*, "One Lion Slain by a Bull and One by a Charge of Shot."
20. *San Francisco Examiner*, "Battle to the Death."
21. *Idaho Statesman*, "Interesting Fair Menagerie."

Chapter 3

22. *Two Republics*, "Just Before the Battle."
23. Beezley, *Judas at the Jockey Club*, 34.
24. *Two Republics*, "How It Happened."
25. *Voz de México*, "Espactáculo Salvaje."
26. *Mexican Herald*, "Other New One."
27. *Mexican Herald*, "Troubles of Billy Clarke."
28. *Mexican Herald*, "Passing Day."
29. *Mexican Herald*, "Troubles of Billy Clarke"; "Billy Smith Hurt."
30. *El Paso Daily Times*, "Mexican Matters."
31. *El Paso Herald*, "Sports and Amusements."
32. *Mexican Herald*, "In a New Role."
33. *Mexican Herald*, "Match Is Off."
34. *Mexican Herald*, "In a New Role."
35. *Mexican Herald*, "Sonora."
36. *Mexican Herald*, "Hanna."
37. *Mexican Herald*, "Clarke and the Grizzly."
38. *Mexican Herald*, "Sick Athlete."
39. *Mexican Herald*, "Clarke in Good Trim."
40. LaFevor, *Prizefighting and Civilization*, 33.
41. *Mexican Herald*, "Sick Athlete."
42. *Mexican Herald*, "Bear, Billy Clarke, and the Cat."
43. *Mexican Herald*, "Was Billy Afraid of the Bull?"
44. *The Gazette*, "Ursus' Fabled Feat."
45. *Quad-City Times*, "Bull Won the Match."
46. Schell, "Lions, Bulls, and Baseball," 266.
47. *Evening Times*, "Blustering Bullfighter."

48. Ibid.
49. Ibid.
50. Ibid.
51. Ibid.
52. *Inter Ocean*, "'Somethin' Doin't.'"
53. *Quad-City Times*, "Bull Won the Match."
54. Ibid.
55. *El Paso Herald*, "Exhibition of Strength."
56. Ibid.
57. *El Paso Herald*, "Concert!"
58. *El Paso Herald*, "Billy Disappointed."
59. *El Paso Herald*, "Showmen Were Mobbed."
60. *Fort Worth Record and Register*, "Mr. Billy Clarke the Strong Man from Peru."
61. *Fort Worth Record and Register*, "Attacked by Angry Mob."
62. *El Paso Herald*, "Showmen Were Mobbed."
63. *Fort Worth Record and Register*, "Attacked by Angry Mob."
64. Ibid.
65. *El Paso Herald*, "Showmen Were Mobbed."
66. Ibid.
67. *Fort Worth Record and Register*, "City News."
68. *Arkansas Democrat*, "Court Notes."
69. *Mexican Herald*, "Billy Clark."
70. *Inter Ocean*, "Says Mr. Rooney to Mr. Clark."
71. Schell, "Lions, Bulls, and Baseball," 266.
72. *El Paso Times*, "Day in the City."
73. Hanes, *Bulldogger*, 63.

Chapter 4

74. Schell, "Lions, Bulls, and Baseball," 266.
75. Ibid., 268.
76. Ibid., 269.
77. Ibid., 269–70.
78. Ibid., 270.
79. *San Francisco Examiner*, "Terrific Fight Between Savage Bull and African Lion."
80. *Los Angeles Evening Post-Record*, "Are Morrison's Lions a Nuisance."

81. *Los Angeles Evening Express*, "Resort that Is a Disgrace to the City."
82. *Los Angeles Times*, "'Blind Pig' in Lions' Den."
83. *Union-Banner*, "He Came to Grief."
84. *El Paso Herald*, "Bull Fight Called Off."
85. *El Paso Times*, "Bull and Lion."
86. *El Paso Times*, "Sunday's Fight."
87. *El Paso Herald*, "Bull and Lion."
88. *St. Andrew's Cross* 16, no. 11, "Letters to the Editor."
89. *Newton Daily Herald*, "Bull Whipped Lion."
90. *San Francisco Examiner*, "Terrific Fight Between Savage Bull and African Lion."
91. *El Paso Daily Times*, "Bloodthirsty El Paso."
92. *Galveston Tribune*, "News Briefed."
93. *El Paso Daily Times*, "Bloodthirsty El Paso."
94. *Newton Daily Herald*, "Bull Whipped Lion."
95. *San Francisco Call*, "Bull and Lion in the Arena."
96. *Cleveland Leader*, "First Authentic Photographs."
97. *El Paso Daily Times*, "Bloodthirsty El Paso."
98. *San Francisco Examiner*, "Terrific Fight Between Savage Bull and African Lion."
99. Ibid.
100. *Newton Daily Herald*, "Bull Whipped Lion."
101. Ibid.
102. *San Francisco Examiner*, "Terrific Fight Between Savage Bull and African Lion."
103. *El Paso Sunday Times*, "Even Los Angeles Enters a Protest."
104. *San Francisco Examiner*, "Terrific Fight Between Savage Bull and African Lion."
105. *El Paso Herald*, "Bull Fights."
106. *Houston Daily Post*, "Exchange Interviews."
107. *Brownsville Herald*, "Fight."
108. *El Paso Times*, "Suicide Made a Society Function."
109. *Newton Daily Herald*, "Bull Whipped Lion."
110. *El Paso Herald*, "Bull Dog vs. Badger."
111. *Evening Mail*, "Tiny Piece of Horseflesh."
112. *Courier-Journal*, "Smallest of Horses Comes to the United States."

Chapter 5

113. *St. Louis Post Dispatch*, "Carleton Bass Tells Dramatic Story."

114. *San Francisco Examiner*, "Love, Heroism, and Murder."

115. *Mexican Herald*, "Bull Fight," April 24, 1899.

116. *Mexican Herald*, "Is No Case."

117. *Mexican Herald*, "Bull Fight," February 21, 1899.

118. *Detroit Free Press*, "They're Women, Yet They Glory in the Gory Sport of Bullfighting."

119. *San Francisco Examiner*, "Love, Heroism, and Murder."

120. *Mexican Herald*, "E. Carleton Bass Kills Cervera."

121. *St. Louis Globe Democrat*, "Says Norris Told Him of Plans to Fleece Public."

122. *Macon Times-Democrat*, "Saw a Bull Fight."

123. Ibid.

124. *Chicago Eagle*, "Spaniard Wants to Introduce Bull-Baiting."

125. *Times-Democrat*, "Protest on Bull Fight."

126. *Akron Beacon*, "Mob Burns Arena at St. Louis."

127. *St. Louis Post Dispatch*, "Bullfight Crowd Burns Pavilion."

128. *Chicago Tribune*, "Riot at Bull Fight."

129. Ibid.

130. *Akron Beacon*, "Mob Burns Arena at St. Louis."

131. *St. Louis Republic*, "Matador Bass Kills Bullfighter."

132. *San Francisco Examiner*, "Love, Heroism, and Murder."

133. Sánchez Soledad, *Historia de Ciudad Juárez a Través de los Toros*, 140.

134. *San Francisco Examiner*, "Her Vow."

135. *Quad-City Times*, "Woman Avenges Her Husband."

136. *Baltimore Sun*, "MME. Cervera's Vow."

137. *Quad-City Times*, "Woman Avenges Her Husband."

138. *St. Louis Republic*, "To Fight Bulls without Harm."

139. Ibid.

140. *St. Louis Globe-Democrat*, "Injunction Is Asked."

141. *St. Louis Post Dispatch*, "Widow of Spanish Victim."

142. *Washington Times*, "Cervera's Widow Assaults Matador."

143. *St. Louis Post-Dispatch*, "Bull Fight Today."

144. *St. Louis Post-Dispatch*, "The Haunted House of the World's Fair."

Chapter 6

145. *Albuquerque Citizen*, "Big Buffalo Defeats Bull Sunday."
146. Draine, *Cowboy Life*, 33.
147. Ibid., 35.
148. *El Paso Times*, "Buffalo."
149. *El Paso Times*, "Last Chance at Buffalo."
150. *El Paso Times*, "To Fight in Mexico City."
151. *El Paso Times*, "U.S. and Mexico Fight."

Chapter 7

152. *New Orleans Times-Picayune*, "French Bull Fighter."
153. *Kansas City Star*, "The Fall of a Bull Fighter."
154. *El Paso Morning Times*, "Felix Robert Returns."
155. *El Paso Times*, "Third Grand Bull Fight."
156. *El Paso Morning Times*, "Wouldn't Take a Dare."
157. *El Paso Herald*, "Felix Robert and His Bull Fight."
158. Ibid.
159. Ibid.
160. *Times Dispatch*, "Women Witness Sickening Sight."
161. *St. Louis Globe-Democrat*, "Matador Gored by Bull: Women Faint at Sight."
162. *Albuquerque Journal*, "Matadors Gored in Juarez Bull Ring."
163. *El Paso Times*, "Buffalo."
164. *El Paso Times*, "Mrs. Fiske."
165. *El Paso Times*, "Best in the Business."
166. *El Paso Herald*, "Mrs. Fisk on the Brutality of the Bull Fight."
167. Ibid.
168. *El Paso Herald*, "Crusade Against Bull Fights in Mexico."
169. *El Paso Herald*, "Badger Fights."
170. *El Paso Herald*, "El Paso's Responsibility and Mexican Bullfights."
171. *El Paso Herald*, "Bullfighter Appeals to the Constitution."
172. Ibid.
173. Ibid.
174. Ibid.
175. *El Paso Herald*, "Mrs. Minnie Fiske Assumes Role of the Bill Boy.

Chapter 8

176. *Albuquerque Citizen*, "Big Buffalo Defeats Bull Sunday."
177. *Albuquerque Journal*, "Matadors Gored in Juarez Bull Ring."
178. *El Paso Morning Times*, "Felix Robert Returns."
179. *El Paso Times*, "Wants to Fight the Tiger."
180. *El Paso Morning Times*, "Amusements," October 14, 1908.
181. *El Paso Times*, "Record Crowd Sees Bull and Tiger Fight."
182. *El Paso Herald*, "Bull Fights Leopard in Juarez Bull Ring."
183. Ibid.
184. *El Paso Times*, "Record Crowd Sees Bull and Tiger Fight."
185. Ibid.
186. Ibid.
187. *Clayton Record*, "Bull and Tiger Fight to the Death."
188. *El Paso Times*, "Tiger Had Arrived in Juarez."
189. *El Paso Times*, "Juarez Bull Ring," January 7, 1909.
190. Ibid.
191. *Bisbee Daily Review*, "Bull and Tiger Fight Sickening Spectacle."
192. Ibid.
193. *El Paso Times*, "Tiger and Bull Battle for Life."
194. Ibid.
195. *The Republic*, "Bull and Tiger Fight."
196. *El Paso Times*, "Americans Did Not Like Fight."
197. *San Antonio Daily Express*, "Bull and Tiger Are Pitted in Ring at Juarez."
198. *El Paso Herald*, "How to Stop the Pullman Tip Nuisance."
199. *El Paso Herald*, "Bull Fights and Humanity."
200. *El Paso Times*, "Bull Fight," January 25, 1909.
201. *El Paso Morning Times*, "Sunday at the Juarez Bull Ring."
202. Ibid.
203. *El Paso Times*, "Amusements," February 5, 1909.
204. *El Paso Times*, "Bull Fight," February 8, 1909.
205. *El Paso Times*, "Bulldogs Fight a Big Bull at Juarez Arena."
206. *El Paso Times*, "Battle Royal to the Death at Juarez Bull Ring."
207. *El Paso Morning Times*, "Sunday at the Juarez Bull Ring," February 13, 1909.
208. *El Paso Times*, "Juarez Bull Ring," February 26, 1909.
209. *El Paso Times*, "Bull Fight," March 1, 1909.
210. *Washington Post*, "Americans Can Find Plenty of Action."
211. *Albuquerque Morning Journal*, "Wild Panic in Bull Ring at Juarez."

212. *Los Angeles Herald*, "Describes Brutality of Some Recent Bull Fights."
213. *El Paso Morning Times*, "France Refused to License Bull Ring."
214. *El Paso Morning Times*, "Felix Robert Returns."
215. *El Paso Herald*, "Mrs. Fiske Says Wage War on the Bull Ring."
216. *El Paso Herald*, "Juarez Will Have Drinking Fountain."

Chapter 9

217. *Democrat and Chronicle*, "Badger Feared by His Mammoth Pets."
218. Tobias, *Behemoth*, 99.
219. Ibid.
220. *Pittsburgh Press*, "Well-What of It?"
221. *Eugene Guard*, "UO Students Bone Up on Tusko's Skeleton."
222. *El Paso Times*, "Juarez Bull Ring," January 29, 1913.
223. *Greensboro Daily Record*, "Bull in a Fight with an Elephant."
224. *El Paso Herald*, "Minister Assails Americans."
225. *Pittsburgh Press*, "Well-What of It?"
226. *El Paso Times*, "Bull-Elephant Fight Is Tame."
227. *Eugene Guard*, "UO Students Bone Up on Tusko's Skeleton."
228. *El Paso Times*, "Bull-Elephant Fight Is Tame."
229. *Eugene Guard*, "UO Students Bone Up on Tusko's Skeleton."
230. *Sunday World Herald*, "Thrillers that Americans Can See."
231. *Eugene Guard*, "UO Students Bone Up on Tusko's Skeleton."
232. *Weekly Town Talk*, "Details of Tusko's Successful 'Bull Fight.'"
233. Ibid.
234. Ibid.
235. *Eugene Guard*, "UO Students Bone Up on Tusko's Skeleton."
236. *Amarillo Daily News*, "Top o' the Morning."
237. *Brazil Daily Times*, "Elephant Bests a Lion."
238. *Weekly Town Talk*, "Details of Tusko's Successful 'Bull Fight.'"
239. Tobias, *Behemoth*, 107–8.
240. Ibid., 109–10.
241. *Eugene Guard*, "UO Students Bone Up on Tusko's Skeleton."
242. Lewis and Fish, *I Loved Rogues*, 8.
243. *Pittsburgh Press*, "Well-What of It?"
244. *New York Daily News*, "Big Top."

Conclusion

245. *El Paso Herald*, "Mrs. Fiske Still Fighting."
246. Ibid.
247. Romo, *Ringside Seat to a Revolution*, 189.

BIBLIOGRAPHY

Newspapers

Akron Beacon. "Mob Burns Arena at St. Louis." June 6, 1904.
Albuquerque Citizen. "Big Buffalo Defeats Bull Sunday." January 29, 1907.
Albuquerque Journal. "Matadors Gored in Juarez Bull Ring." July 15, 1907.
———. "Would Deprive Mexico of National Pastime." January 30, 1907.
Albuquerque Morning Journal. "Ladies." April 6, 1903.
———. "Wild Panic in Bull Ring at Juarez." July 18, 1909.
Amarillo Daily News. "Top o' the Morning." February 4, 1913.
Anadarko Daily Democrat. "A Frightful Sport." April 17, 1902.
Argus-Leader (Sioux Falls, SD). "Buffalo Fights Bull." January 29, 1907.
Arkansas Democrat (Little Rock). "Court Notes." September 17, 1900.
———. "News of all the Courts." September 10, 1900.
———. "Rutland Foreman." September 24, 1900.
Atchison Daily Champion. "Taft and Diaz Meet on the International Bridge."
    October 16, 1909.
Atlanta Constitution. "His Bulls Wouldn't Fight." February 4, 1907.
Baltimore Sun. "MME. Cervera's Vow." July 31, 1904.
———. "Widow Home with Dead." June 12, 1904.
Bangor Daily News. "Minnie Maddern Fiske Comments on Lindy at the Bull
    Fight." December 19, 1927.
Bisbee Daily Review. "Bull and Tiger Fight Sickening Spectacle." January 16,
    1909.

Bloomington Leader. "Mangled by Lions." February 15, 1894.

The Brand (Hereford, TX). "Like Days of Nero." April 4, 1902.

Brazil Daily Times, (Brazil, IN). "Elephant Bests a Lion." February 3, 1913.

Brownsville Herald. "A Fight." April 17, 1902.

Buffalo Evening News. "Fitz's Lion Nero." January 30, 1896.

Calgary Herald. "C.M.R. Sports Saturday." June 28, 1905.

Carlsbad Current-Argus. "Underdog Bull Defeats Tiger in Blood-Spattered Reynosa." February 4, 1958.

Chattanooga Daily Times. "No Bull Fight in New Orleans." October 25, 1904.

Chicago Eagle. "A Spaniard Wants to Introduce Bull-Baiting." September 17, 1902.

Chicago Tribune. "Riot at Bull Fight." June 6, 1904.

Chippewa Herald-Telegram (Chippewa Falls, WI). "Commodore Wouldn't Wrestle." May 24, 1894.

Cincinnati Enquirer. "Bull and Buffalo in a Fierce Battle." February 5, 1907.

———. "Prof. Boone." May 18, 1898.

Circleville News. "Bull Versus Bear." May 23, 1895.

Clayton Record. "Bull and Tiger Fight to the Death." October 23, 1908.

Cleveland Leader. "First Authentic Photographs and Complete Story of the Encounter Between an African Lion and a Fierce Bull." May 11, 1902.

El Correo Español (Mexico City). "La Contienda de Box en Pachuca." November 28, 1895.

Courier-Journal (Louisville, KY). "King of Beasts." February 5, 1898.

———. "Smallest of Horses Comes to the United States." February 15, 1903.

Courier-News (Bridgewater, NJ). "Tourists Blamed for Bull Fights." August 11, 1908.

Daily Advocate (Victoria, TX). "Bull Fighter Retires." July 15, 1905.

———. "A Fighting Mule." April 28, 1902.

Daily Arkansas Gazette (Little Rock). "Clark in Trouble." September 23, 1900.

Daily Tribune (Salt Lake City). "Veterans of the Midway." September 27, 1901.

Dayton Herald. "The Nemisis of Her Husband's Slayer." June 27, 1904.

Decatur News. "Bull and Bullets." June 8, 1900.

Democrat and Chronicle Democrat and Chronicle (Rochester, NY). "Badger Feared by His Mammoth Pets." July 7, 1901.

———. "Must Be They're Envious." March 23, 1909.

Denver Post. "The Lion and the Grizzly." August 27, 1902.

Detroit Free Press. "They're Women, Yet They Glory in the Gory Sport of Bullfighting." May 31, 1903.

El Diario (Mexico City). "El Buen Tono." April 4, 1904.

El Diario del Hogar (Mexico City). "El Pugilato en Pachuca." November 27, 1895.

El Paso Daily Times. "Bloodthirsty El Paso." April 25, 1902.

———. "Mexican Matters." October 18, 1896.

El Paso Evening Post. "League Indorses Two Amendments." July 16, 1929.

El Paso Herald. "At the Bull Fight." May 24, 1909.

———. "Badger Fights." July 19, 1907.

———. "Best of the Season." October 5, 1905.

———. "Billy Disappointed." July 25, 1900.

———. "Brutal Juarez 'Sport'." January 12, 1909.

———. "Buffalo-Bull Fight to be Held in Barcelona, Spain." June 13, 1908.

———. "Buffalo Donated to the City by Felix Robert." April 6, 1907.

———. "Buffalo Fight Proves Fiasco." February 4, 1907.

———. "Buffalo to Spain." June 17, 1908.

———. "Bull and Lion." April 10, 1902.

———. "Bull Dog vs. Badger." June 21, 1902.

———. "Bull Fight Called Off." April 7, 1902.

———. "Bull Fights and Humanity." January 19, 1909.

———. "Bull Fights." April 18, 1902.

———. "Bullfights in Mexico and American Patronage." January 11, 1908.

———. "Bullfighter Appeals to the Constitution." January 25, 1908.

———. "Bull Fight for Thursday of Congress Week." October 5, 1905.

———. "Bull Fights Leopard in Juarez Bull Ring." October 19, 1908.

———. "Circus Day Brings Tented City of Novel Acts to El Paso Today." September 2, 1929.

———. "City Will Accept Buffalo Present." April 8, 1907.

———. "Concert!" July 19, 1900.

———. "Crusade Against Bull Fights in Mexico." February 26, 1908.

———. "Dr. Samaniego of Juarez Is Critically Ill." September 29, 1905.

———. "Elephants Take a Walk." February 5, 1913.

———. "El Paso's Responsibility and Mexican Bullfights." December 3, 1907.

———. "Exhibition of Strength." July 16, 1900.

———. "Federal Building Notes." June 20, 1908.

———. "Felix Robert and His Bull Fight." August 17, 1905.

———. "Felix Robert Wants to Be American." January 29, 1908.

———. "'First Out' in the Theater and Mrs. Fiske's Idea." May 13, 1907.

———. "Friday, Jan. 24." December 31, 1908.

———. "Had Brass Knuckles." June 28, 1900.

———. "How to Stop the Pullman Tip Nuisance." January 12, 1909.

———. "Juarez Still Guarded." December 26, 1910.

———. "Juarez Will Have Drinking Fountain." April 23, 1910.

———. "Laura Baker on Trial for Theft." February 8, 1902.

———. "Minister Assails Americans." February 3, 1913.

———. "Mrs. Minnie Fiske Assumes Role of the Bill Boy." June 18, 1908.

———. "Mrs. Fisk on the Brutality of the Bull Fight." November 9, 1907.

———. "Mrs. Fiske Says Wage War on the Bull Ring." September 3, 1910.

———. "Mrs. Fiske Still Fighting Against Mexican Bull Fights." January 7, 1914.

———. "Negro Bull Wrestler." June 22, 1900.

———. "Paris, France, Woman Files Damage Suit in Court Here." February 23, 1928.

———. "Plan Rush Battle Continues." May 9, 1911.

———. "Possibility of Prize Fights Over in Juarez." April 23, 1903.

———. "Probably Another Big Fake Tomorrow." April 12, 1902.

———. "The Showmen Were Mobbed." August 6, 1900.

———. "Sports and Amusements." February 5, 1897.

———. "Wild Bulls with Police Escort to Parade." August 12, 1905.

———. "Will Be a Big Fight." March 3, 1906.

———. "Woman Gets Back Property Given to Husband by Duress." May 25, 1927.

El Paso Morning Times. "Amusements." February 25, 1909.

———. "Amusements." October 14, 1908.

———. "Farewell Bull Fight." October 22, 1906.

———. "Felix Robert." December 25, 1904.

———. "Felix Robert Returns" September 18, 1908.

———. "France Refused to License Bull Ring." April 10, 1911.

———. "Hector McLean." December 30, 1912.

———. "Morenito Chico, Matador, Gored." September 2, 1907.

———. "Personal." June 6, 1911.

———. "Sunday at the Juarez Bull Ring." February 11, 1909.

———. "Sunday at the Juarez Bull Ring." February 13, 1909.

———. "Will Have Bull Fight Parade." January 17, 1908.

———. "Wouldn't Take a Dare." April 6, 1905.

El Paso Times. "Americans Did Not Like Fight." January 11, 1909.

———. "Amusements." February 5, 1909.

———. "Amusements." February 7, 1909.

————. "At the Juarez Bull Ring Sunday." February 20, 1909.

————. "A Battle Royal to the Death at Juarez Bull Ring." February 9, 1909.

————. "The Best in the Business." May 31, 1907.

————. "Better Banderillero." April 3, 1905.

————. "Betting Odds Favor the Lion." April 12, 1902.

————. "Bound by Ties of Strongest." March 23, 1905.

————. "The Buffalo." April 29, 1907.

————. "Buffalo Against Bull." January 18, 1907.

————. "Buffalo for the City." April 6, 1907.

————. "The Bull and the Lion." April 8, 1902.

————. "Bull and Bear Fight." April 9, 1902.

————. "Bull and Lion." April 9, 1902.

————. "Bulldogs Fight a Big Bull at Juarez Arena, February 15, 1909.

————. "Bull-Elephant Fight Is Tame." February 3, 1913.

————. "The Bull Fight." February 8, 1909.

————. "The Bull Fight." January 11, 1909.

————. "The Bull Fight." January 25, 1909.

————. "The Bull Fight." March 1, 1909.

————. "Bull Fights Buffalo." April 27, 1908.

————. "A Day in the City." March 11, 1902.

————. "Even Los Angeles Enters a Protest." April 20, 1902.

————. "Felix Robert to Wed Today." April 30, 1908.

————. "Fighters of Tayahua." February 19, 1907.

————. "Four Fierce Bulls." March 18, 1907.

————. "Grand Bull Fight at Juarez Bull Ring." January 1, 1909.

————. "Grand Tiger and Bull Fight at Juarez Bull Ring Next Sunday." January 6, 1909.

————. "Grand Wrestling Match." January 22, 1909.

————. "Illinois Newspaper Tells About Juarez Bull Fights." January 31, 1909.

————. "Juarez Bull Ring." February 26, 1909.

————. "Juarez Bull Ring." January 7, 1909.

————. "Juarez Bull Ring." January 28, 1913.

————. "Juarez Bull Ring." January 29, 1913.

————. "Jury Releases Bull Fighters." September 17, 1904.

————. "Last Chance at Buffalo." May 11, 1907.

————. "Leaves Bondsman to Hold the Bag." March 12, 1902.

————. "Lion Will Be Fed on Water." April 17, 1902.

————. "Mrs. Fiske." May 31, 1907.

———. "Pitiful Spectacle." April 15, 1902.

———. "Protest Against Bull Fighting." April 13, 1902.

———. "Record Crowd Sees Bull and Tiger Fight." October 19, 1908.

———. "Robert Purchases Tiger from Trainer Hagenback." December 15, 1908.

———. "Signs a Contract." July 8, 1905.

———. "Suicide Made a Society Function." April 23, 1902.

———. "Sunday's Fight." April 10, 1902.

———. "Third Grand Bull Fight." March 4, 1905.

———. "Tiger and Bull Battle for Life." January 11, 1909.

———. "The Tiger Had Arrived in Juarez." January 1, 1909.

———. "To Fight in Mexico City." June 26, 1907.

———. "To Prevent Fight." January 31, 1907.

———. "U.S. and Mexico Fight." April 10, 1908.

———. "Wants to Fight the Tiger." September 23, 1908.

Emery County Progress (Castle Dale, UT). "Buffalo Bests Bull in Desperate Fight." March 2, 1907.

Eugene Guard. "UO Students Bone Up on Tusko's Skeleton." March 20, 1955.

Evansville Journal. "Buffalo in a Bull Fight." February 1, 1907.

Evening Mail (Stockton, CA). "Tiny Piece of Horseflesh." December 27, 1902.

Evening News (Paterson, NJ). "Beasts in the Arena." May 8, 1895.

Evening Sun. "Minnie Maddern Fiske Asks Yale Protest on Bull Fight." November 21, 1930.

Evening Telegram. "The End!" August 1, 1911.

Evening Times (Washington, D.C.). "A Blustering Bullfighter." July 26, 1900.

Fort Scott Daily Monitor. "Fitz's Pet Lion Killed." April 18, 1896.

Fort Worth Record and Register. "Attacked by Angry Mob." August 2, 1900.

———. "City News." August 3, 1900.

———. "Clarke, the Giant." August 5, 1900.

———. "Mr. Billy Clarke the Strong Man from Peru." July 29, 1900.

Galveston Daily News. "Editor as Bull Fighter." April 25, 1905.

Galveston Tribune. "The News Briefed." April 14, 1902.

The Gazette (York, PA). "Ursus' Fabled Feat." February 28, 1898.

Greensboro Daily Record. "Bull in a Fight with an Elephant." August 5, 1913.

Hartford Courant. "Bull and Buffalo." February 9, 1907.

———. "Here Is Real Sport." April 3, 1909.

Herald and Review (Decatur, IL). "Taylorville News Notes." March 8, 1909.

Hollis Times (Hollis, NH). "A Bull Fight in Mexico." May 8, 1914.

Houston Daily Post. "Exchange Interviews." April 20, 1902.

Idaho Statesman (Boise). "Down in San Francisco." March 23, 1894.

———. "Interesting Fair Menagerie." September 13, 1901.

Illinois State Register (Springfield). "Grizzly Bested Lion." September 20, 1902.

The Inquirer (Owensboro, KY). "Animal Combat." February 12, 1905.

Inter Ocean (Chicago). "Says Mr. Rooney to Mr. Clark." April 19, 1901.

———. "'Somethin' Doin't'" April 18, 1901.

———. "Victim of a Vicious Lion." April 16, 1895.

Iola Register. "Lion Parnell Killed." May 10, 1895.

The Journal (Meriden, CT). "Texas Bull Fights Buffaloes in Ring." January 28, 1907.

Journal-Gazette (West Plains, MO). "There Will Be No More Bull Fights." September 22, 1904.

Kansas City Star. "The Fall of a Bull Fighter." February 24, 1907.

Kansas Weekly Capital (Topeka, KS). "Killed 400 Bulls." April 5, 1904.

Kenosha News. "Aspirant in to Win." January 27, 1902.

———. "Athletic Exhibition." February 3, 1902.

Kiowa County Times (Greensburg, KS). "A Large Fierce Grizzly." March 30, 1894.

Laredo Weekly Times. "Anti-Bull Fight Movement." October 16, 1910.

Le Monde (Paris). "Court in Mexico City Permanently Bans Bullfighting in the Capital." June 18, 2022.

Lima Morning Star and Republican-Gazette. "'Band of Mercy' Is Making Havana a Paradise for Animals." December 15, 1912.

Los Angeles Evening Express. "The Lions' Den Is Again in Trouble." October 20, 1900.

———. "Lobengula for Sale But City Cannot Buy." March 23, 1905.

———. "Los Angeles Lion's Battle." April 14, 1902.

———. "Resort that Is a Disgrace to the City." March 25, 1901.

Los Angeles Evening Post-Record. "Are Morrison's Lions a Nuisance." August 9, 1900.

———. "Lion Is Victor of Many Bull Fights." December 19, 1902.

Los Angeles Herald. "Describes Brutality of Some Recent Bull Fights." September 21, 1909.

———. "French Matador Explains Bull Fighting to Jeff." August 18, 1905.

———. "Lion and Bear." April 24, 1894.

———. "Loben Gula and Keeper Rice." June 23, 1905.

———. "Matador Will Take Chances." July 8, 1906.

———. "Parnell and the Bear." April 16. 1894.

————. "Possible Addition to Eastlake Park Zoo." June 23, 1905.

————. "Senorita Awaits News from the Ring." July 15, 1906.

————. "Tammany's Topical Talks." May 27, 1894.

Los Angeles Times. "'Blind Pig' in Lions' Den." November 11, 1900.

————. "Bull's Chance." September 5, 1909.

————. "He-Cow Fighting Tame as Ping Pong." July 29, 1906.

————. "Lions' Den Case." April 7, 1901.

————. "Lions Den Raided." August 9, 1900.

————. "Lion Tales Differ." December 12, 1909.

————. "Parnell Killed." May 6, 1895.

————. "Same Old Lions." August 21, 1900.

————. "Summary of the Day." October 24, 1900.

————. "Summary of the Day." October 28, 1900.

Macon Times-Democrat (Macon, MO). "Saw a Bull Fight." December 24, 1903.

Mexican Herald (Mexico City). "At San Bartolo." March 31, 1898.

————. "The Bear, Billy Clarke, and the Cat." January 3, 1898.

————. "Billy Clark." November 24, 1900.

————. "Billy Clarke Opens a New Athletic Club." October 4, 1898.

————. "Billy's Show." December 25, 1897.

————. "Billy Smith Hurt." April 24, 1901.

————. "Bucareli Bull Ring." July 18, 1897.

————. "Buffalo Does Not Fight." February 5, 1907.

————. "The Bull Fight." April 24, 1899.

————. "The Bull Fight." September 6, 1897.

————. "Clarke and the Grizzly." November 9, 1897.

————. "Clarke in Good Trim." October 20, 1895.

————. "Clarke Replies." June 26, 1897.

————. "Clark in Effigy." September 4, 1897.

————. "Deposit Returned." October 7, 1897.

————. "E. Carleton Bass Kills Cervera." June 10, 1904.

————. "Hanna." April 22, 1898.

————. "In a New Role." December 23, 1897.

————. "In Trouble Again." July 13, 1897.

————. "Is No Case." October 18, 1898.

————. "Items of Interest from All Over the World." September 1, 1907.

————. "Match Is Off." July 1, 1899.

————. "No Show." December 27, 1897.

————. "Object to the Fight." March 11, 1909.

————. "The Olympic Club Entertainment." September 27, 1896.

————. "Other New One." June 12, 1899.

————. "Pachuca Notes." June 25, 1899.

————. "Passing Day." June 23, 1896.

————. "Planchette." June 11, 1899.

————. "Prize Fighting Unknown Sport in Mexico." June 12, 1904.

————. "Puebla News." January 8, 1898.

————. "Romulus-Clarke." July 4, 1897.

————. "A Sick Athlete." March 3, 1898.

————. "Sonora." January 8, 1898.

————. "Suicide of Billy Clark." April 7, 1898.

————. "The Troubles of Billy Clarke." October 8, 1896.

————. "Was Billy Afraid of the Bull?" August 27, 1897.

Minneapolis Daily Times. "Called It a Fake." May 23, 1894.

The Monitor (McAllen, TX). "Border Promoters Reluctant to Stage Another Tiger-Bull Fiasco." January 30, 1958.

El Monitor Republicano (Mexico City). "Nuevo Combate Pugilistico." November 28, 1895.

————. "Sobre El Combate Pugilistico en Pachuca." November 27, 1895.

Morning Call (San Francisco). "From the Arena." February 17, 1894.

————. "Lion and Bear Fight." May 2, 1894.

Nebraska State Journal (Lincoln). "Hard Life of a Lion Tamer." July 6, 1891.

New Orleans Times-Picayune. "French Bull Fighter." October 23, 1904.

News Tribune (Tacoma, WA). "This Evening." April 21, 1894.

Newton Daily Herald. "Bull Whipped Lion." May 31, 1902.

New York Daily News. "Big Top." April 13, 1933.

New York Times. "Buffalo Defeats Bull." January 28, 1907.

Olney Times. "Great Fight." February 13, 1808.

Our Dumb Animals. "Dumb Friends in Turbulent Mexico." July 1914.

————. "If Madero Is President." September 1911.

————. "In Mexico." September 1911.

————. "Mrs. Minnie Maddern Fiske." August 1908.

————. "New Humane Journal." June 1910.

————. "'Rebels' Stop Bull-Fights." August 1911.

————. "To Deal with Bullies." June 1908.

————. "What Do You Consider." June 1908.

Oxford Courier. "Felix Robert." July 20, 1906.

Philadelphia Inquirer. "The Adam Forepaugh Shows." April 12, 1891.

————. "Forepaugh's Shows." April 19, 1891.

———. "Would Prohibit Sailors from Bull Fight Arenas." October 21, 1921.

Pittsburgh Press. "Well-What of It?" May 25, 1932.

Press Herald (Pine Grove, PA). "Had a Private Bull Fight." April 22, 1898.

Press-Telegram (Long Beach, CA). "Matador Gored by Bull." April 15, 1907.

Quad-City Times (Davenport, IA). "The Bull Won the Match." July 2, 1900.

———. "Woman Avenges Her Husband." June 28, 1904.

Record-Union (Sacramento). "Sensation at the Fair." March 3, 1894.

The Register (Adelaide, SA). "A Bull Fights Two Tigers." January 18, 1909.

Reno Gazette-Journal. "Mexico Has First Ring Battle in Many Years." May 20, 1912.

The Republic (Columbus, IN). "Bull and Tiger Fight." February 25, 1909.

Reynolds's Newspaper (London). "Death of Lobengula." February 18, 1894.

Rock Island Argus. "Fighters Go 20 Rounds in Juarez Bull Ring." May 20, 1912.

San Antonio Daily Express. "Bull and Tiger Are Pitted in Ring at Juarez." January 11, 1909.

San Francisco Call. "Bull and Lion in the Arena." April 14, 1902.

———. "Parnell Fights a Bear." April 2, 1895.

———. "Roosevelt Scored by Noted Actress for African Hunt." June 11, 1909.

———. "Southern Pacific Refuses to Haul a Caged Lion." August 20, 1903.

San Francisco Examiner. "Battle to the Death." May 1, 1895.

———. "Bear and Lion Before the Camera." April 7, 1895.

———. "Her Vow." August 7, 1904.

———. "The Lion They Cannot Tame." May 21, 1894.

———. "Love, Heroism, and Murder." July 3, 1904.

———. "One Lion Slain by a Bull and One by a Charge of Shot." May 6, 1895.

———. "Parnell Again Tastes Blood." April 12, 1895.

———. "Parnell Whipped by a Bull." April 23, 1895.

———. "Sandow and the Tawny King." May 23, 1894.

———. "Terrific Fight Between Savage Bull and African Lion and the Owner of the Latter Is Threatened with Arrest." April 14, 1902.

Santa Cruz Surf. "Justice on a Vacation." August 25, 1903.

El Siglo Diez y Nueve (Mexico City). "El Combate de Pugilistas en Pachuca No Fué Legal." November 28, 1895.

———. "El Nuevo Espectáculo." November 26, 1895.

Spokesman-Review (Spokane, WA). "And T.R. Was Not There." July 18, 1909.

St. Andrew's Cross. "Letters to the Editor." August 1902.

St. Louis Globe-Democrat. "Bull Fight Called Off." June 1, 1902.

———. "Charge Is Misdemeanor." September 11, 1904.

———. "Injunction Is Asked." September 10, 1904.

———. "Lion and Bear Will Not Meet." February 2, 1895.

———. "Matador Gored by Bull: Women Faint at Sight." April 15, 1907.

———. "Says Norris Told Him of Plans to Fleece Public." June 7, 1904.

St. Louis Post Dispatch. "Bullfight Crowd Burns Pavilion." June 6, 1904.

———. "Bull Fight Today." September 18, 1904.

———. "Carleton Bass Tells Dramatic Story." June 9, 1904.

———. "The Haunted House of the World's Fair." November 6, 1904.

———. "Lion Kills Trainer." October 3, 1898.

———. "Matador's Body Is Taken East." June 10, 1904.

———. "Widow of Spanish Victim of American Matador Attacks Felix Robert, Clayton Defendant, with a Dagger." September 16, 1904.

St. Louis Republic. "Matador Bass Kills Bullfighter." June 9, 1904.

———. "To Fight Bulls without Harm." June 11, 1904.

———. "2,000 Spectators Witness Bullfight in the County." September 5, 1904.

———. "Warrants for Bull Fighters." August 3, 1902.

The Sun. "Bull Kills Tiger." October 19, 1908.

Sunday World Herald (Omaha, NE). "Thrillers that Americans Can See Just Across the Rio Grande River." December 13, 1914.

Tacoma Daily Ledger. "Lion Creates Panic during Bull Fight." July 18, 1909.

The Times (Shreveport, LA). "Hand to Horn Battle with an Enraged Bull." February 20, 1910.

Times-Democrat (New Orleans). "A Lion Tamer's Arm Badly Mangled." April 12, 1895.

———. "Protest on Bull Fight." June 5, 1904.

———. "Women at Home and Abroad." June 7, 1908.

Times Dispatch (Richmond). "Women Witness Sickening Sight." November 18, 1905.

Two Republics (Mexico City) "The Bull Ring." April 25, 1900.

———. "How It Happened." November 27, 1895.

———. "Just Before the Battle." November 23, 1895.

———. "To the Rescue." November 2, 1895.

Union-Banner (Clanton, AL). "He Came to Grief." April 3, 1902.

Voz de México (Mexico City) "Espactáculo Salvaje." November 26, 1895.

Washington Post. "Americans Can Find Plenty of Action and Romance." December 11, 1910.

———. "The Last Bullfight? Mexico City Weighs a Ban." December 14, 2021.

Washington Times. "Cervera's Widow Assaults Matador." September 17, 1904.

Weekly Town Talk (Alexandria, LA). "Details of Tusko's Successful 'Bull Fight' in Juarez Arena; Alexandrian Has Part." July 25, 1931.

Books, Dissertations and Journal Articles

Alexander, Shana. *The Astonishing Elephant*. New York: Random House, 2000.

Balleisen, Edward J. *Fraud: An American History from Barnum to Madoff*. Princeton, NJ: Princeton University Press, 2018.

Beezley, William H. *Judas at the Jockey Club and Other Episodes of Porfirian Mexico*. Lincoln: University of Nebraska Press, 2018.

Binns, Archie. *Mrs. Fiske and the American Theatre*. New York: Crown Publishers, 1955.

Brands, H.W. *Leviathan: The Triumph of American Capitalism, 1865–1900*. New York: Anchor Books, 2011.

Campbell, Randolph B. *Gone to Texas: A History of the Lone Star State*. 3rd ed. New York: Oxford University Press, 2017.

Cantrell, Gregg. *The People's Revolt: Texas Populists and the Roots of American Liberalism*. New Haven, CT: Yale University Press, 2020.

Cervera y Topete, Pascual. *Views of Admiral Cervera Regarding the Spanish Navy in the Late War*. Washington, D.C.: U.S. Government Printing Office, 1898.

Cunfer, Geoff, and Bill Waiser, eds. *Bison and People on the North American Great Plains*. College Station: Texas A&M University Press, 2016.

Dickson, Jim. "Buffalo 4, Bulls 0." *Plains Anthropologist* 41, no. 158 (November 1996).

Draine, Cathie, ed. *Cowboy Life: The Letters of George Philip*. Pierre: South Dakota State Historical Society Press, 2007.

Flandrau, Charles Macomb. *Viva Mexico!* Urbana: University of Illinois Press, 1964.

Flores, Dan. "Reviewing an Iconic Story: Environmental History and the Demise of the Bison." In Cunfer and Waiser, *Bison and People on the North American Great Plains*.

Folsom, Bradley. "An Interesting and Odd Present: Transporting American Bison Across the Atlantic in the Eighteenth Century." *Southwestern Historical Quarterly* 120 (July 2016).

Frank, Patrick. *Posada's Broadsheets: Mexican Popular Imagery*. Albuquerque: University of New Mexico Press, 1998.

Frisbee, Margaret. "The Fight of the Century: The Regulation and Reform of Prizefighting in Progressive Era America." PhD diss., University of New Mexico, Albuquerque, 2010.

Hanes, Baily C. *Bill Pickett: Bulldogger*. Norman: University of Oklahoma Press, 1977.

Harris, Charles H., III, and Louis R. Sadler. *The Secret War in El Paso: Mexican Revolutionary Intrigue, 1906–1920*. Albuquerque: University of New Mexico Press, 2009.

Harrison-Kahan, Lori, and Karen E.H. Skinazi. "Miriam Michelson's Yellow Journalism and the Multi-Ethnic West." *MELUS* 40, no. 2 (2015).

Herring, George C. *From Colony to Superpower: U.S. Foreign Relations Since 1776*. New York: Oxford University Press, 2008.

Isenberg, Andrew C. "The Returns of the Bison: Nostalgia, Profit, and Preservation." *Environmental History* 2, no. 2 (1997).

Jiménez Ruiz, Orlando. "En el Ring de la Historia." *Artes de México* 119 (2015).

Johns, Michael. *The City of Mexico in the Age of Díaz*. Austin: University of Texas Press, 1997.

LaFevor, David. *Prizefighting and Civilization: A Cultural History of Boxing, Race, and Masculinity in Mexico and Cuba, 1840–1940*. Albuquerque: University of New Mexico Press, 2020.

LeCompte, Mary Lou. "Pickett, William." Handbook of Texas Online, updated January 7, 2021. https://www.tshaonline.org/handbook/entries/pickett-william.

Lee, Wayne C. *Scotty Philip, the Man Who Saved the Buffalo*. Caldwell, ID: Caxton, 1975.

Lewis, George "Slim," and Byron Fish. *I Loved Rogues: The Life of an Elephant Tramp*. Seattle, WA: Superior Publishing Company, 1978.

Lister, Florence C., and Robert H. Lister. *Chihuahua Storehouse of Storms*. Albuquerque: University of New Mexico Press, 1966.

Lott, Dale F. *American Bison: A Natural History*. Berkeley: University of California Press, 2002.

Pavlik, Steve. "Rohonas and Spotted Lions: The Historical and Cultural Occurrence of the Jaguar, *Panthera onca*, Among the Native Tribes of the American Southwest." *Wicazo Sa Review* 18, no. 1 (Spring 2003).

Pierce, Dale. *Wild West Characters*. Phoenix, AZ: Golden West Publishers, 1991.

Pomerantz, Sidney I. "The Press of a Greater New York, 1898–1900." *New York History* 39, no. 1 (1958).

Quirk, Robert E. *The Mexican Revolution, 1914–1915*. New York: Citadel Press, 1963.

Roberts, Randy. *Papa Jack: Jack Johnson and the Era of White Hopes*. New York: Free Press, 1985.

Robinson, James M. *West from Fort Pierre: The Wild World of James (Scotty) Philip*. Tucson, AZ: Westernlore Publications, 1974.

Romo, David Dorado. *Ringside Seat to a Revolution: An Underground Cultural History of El Paso and Juárez, 1893–1923*. El Paso, TX: Cinco Punto Press, 2005.

Sammons, Jeffrey T. *Beyond the Ring: The Role of Boxing in American Society*. Chicago: University of Illinois Press, 1990.

Sánchez Soledad, José Mario. *Historia de Ciudad Juárez a Través de los Toros*. N.p.: self-published, Kindle, 2021.

Schell, William, Jr. "Lions, Bulls, and Baseball: Colonel R.C. Pate and Modern Sports Promotion in Mexico." *Journal of Sport History* 20, no. 3 (Winter 1993).

Shubert, Adrian. *Death and Money in the Afternoon: A History of Spanish Bullfighting*. New York: Oxford University Press, 1999.

Storer, Tracy I., and Lloyd P. Tevis Jr. *California Grizzly*. Berkeley: University of California Press, 1996.

Streible, Dan. "A History of the Boxing Film, 1894–1915: Social Control and Social Reform in the Progressive Era." *Film History* 3, no. 3 (1989).

Synopsis of the Laws Passed by the Twenty-Second Legislature of the State of Texas. Ann Arbor: University of Michigan Press, 1891.

Szasz, Ferenc Morton. "Scots in the North American West." *Montana: The Magazine of Western History* 51, no. 1 (2001).

Thompson, Hunter S. *Hey Rube: Blood Sport, the Bush Doctrine, and the Downward Spiral of Dumbness*. New York: Simon & Schuster, 2004.

Tobias, Ronald B. *Behemoth: The History of the Elephant in America*. New York: Harper Collins, 2013.

Tutino, John. *From Insurrection to Revolution in Mexico: Social Bases of Agrarian Violence, 1750–1940*. Princeton, NJ: Princeton University Press, 1986.

Vehlahn, Nancy. *The Buffalo King: The Story of Scotty Philip*. New York: Scribner, 1971.

Walton, Homer C. "The M.L. Clark Wagon Show." *Bandwagon* 9, no. 2 (March–April 1965).

————. "Ned and Mena, Famous Elephants." *Bandwagon* 2, No. 6 (November–December 1958.

White, Owen. *Out of the Desert: The Historical Romance of El Paso*. El Paso, TX: McMath Company, 1923.

White, Richard. *The Republic for Which It Stands: The United States during Reconstruction and the Gilded Age, 1865–1896*. New York: Oxford University Press, 2017.

Wilentz, Sean. "America's Lost Egalitarian Tradition." *Daedalus* 131, no. 1 (2002).

INDEX

A

Adam Forepaugh Circus. *See*
circuses: Adam Forepaugh
Circus
American buffalo. *See* bison
American Society for the
Prevention of Cruelty to
Animals. *See* animal rights
activists: ASPCA
animal fights, laws against 11, 21,
22, 74, 86, 108, 109, 121,
140, 142. *See also* interspecies
fights
Animal Protection Association of
Mexico. *See* animal rights
activists: Animal Protection
Association of Mexico
animal rights activists 140. *See
also* journalism's evolution
and influence on newspapers 65,
108, 116, 134, 140

and religious element 106, 109,
130
Animal Protection Association of
Mexico 124
ASPCA 11, 21, 48, 82, 86, 120,
122, 140, 141
in California 21
in Cuba 122
in Europe 101
influencing public opinion 108,
110
in Mexico 119, 122, 140
in Missouri 75, 81, 82, 102
in New Orleans 82, 102
International Humane Society
106
in Texas 11, 94, 97, 105, 111,
120, 121, 122
Mexican SPCA 110
Art of the Toreador, The 103. *See
also* Robert, Felix

ABOUT THE AUTHOR

Bradley Folsom is an award-winning author and history professor who specializes in the Texas-Mexico borderlands. He enjoys true crime and solving historical mysteries.